The Purple Kiwi Cookbook

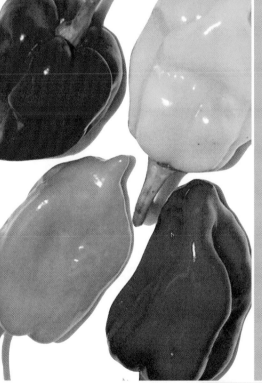

ENJOY
PREPARING
AND LEARNING
ABOUT SOME
OF THE WORLD'S
MOST EXOTIC
PRODUCE

BY KAREN CAPLAN

The Purple Kiwi Cookbook

Published by Karen Caplan, Frieda's®, Inc.

Copyright © 2001

Frieda's, Inc.
P.O. Box 58488
Los Angeles, California 90058
www.friedas.com

Library of Congress Number: 00-134957

ISBN: 0-9703226-0-7

Designed, Edited, and Manufactured by

Favorite Recipes® Press

An imprint of

FRP

P.O. Box 305142

Nashville, Tennessee 37230

1-800-358-0560

Manufactured in the United States of America

PREFACE

Good morning!

I have to start the introduction to my cookbook by saying "Good morning," because that's how I've started all my letters to friends for the past twenty-six years.

KAREN CAPLAN

The genesis of this cookbook really began when I was a small child. When I was a baby, my mom wanted to find a job that would allow her to have flexible hours so that she could breast-feed me (I know it sounds corny, but that's what she says). She called my dad's aunt and uncle, who worked at the produce market in Los Angeles, because she had heard they had crazy hours. Since their bookkeeper had quit that day, they offered my mom a job on the spot!

Mom started cashiering, and one day she noticed a small stack of mushrooms next to her cashier stand that no one seemed to be paying attention to. So, she took it upon herself to sell them. Funny thing, a few days later more mushrooms appeared. So, she sold them. And it kept happening; more mushrooms, more sales. She suddenly was thrust into the sales department and loved it!

Unable to find enough mushrooms to supply her growing customer base, she did something really wild and unheard of. She loaded me into her station wagon, and we drove around Southern California visiting mushroom farmers. Visiting growers? No one at the produce market had ever thought of that before. Mom developed a great reputation for her "personal touch," and actually, it was those mushroom growers who later enabled Mom to launch her own company. (As an aside, Mom was pregnant with my sister Jackie during our mushroom treks, so as a young child, Jackie was known as the "mushroom baby.")

My earliest memory of my mom's business was the sweet aroma of fruits—not mushrooms. My mom worked long hours (she left our house at 1:30 A.M., kissing both of us before departing, and returned around 5:00 P.M., in time for dinner). Every day, when she came through the door, she always had a wonderful aroma of tropical fruit and citrus. I can still remember hugging her and smelling the "eau de mango-papaya-pineapple-grapefruit."

FRIEDA CAPLAN

I started working with Mom at the age of ten (stuffing envelopes) and eventually began working summers when I was old enough. When I decided I wanted to work with Mom at her company, she was pleasantly surprised. She had never expected either Jackie or me to join her. I quickly realized I shared Mom's philosophy—the work we did had to be fun, and the products we decided to introduce and sell had to taste good.

Over the years, we've had a tremendous amount of good luck and great timing. For example, everyone is always curious as to how we chose the color purple as our company color.

Well, I could tell you that we selected the color purple after doing extensive marketing research on the color that

FRIEDA CAPLAN, FOUNDER OF FRIEDA'S, INC., RECEIVES A LARGE AIR SHIPMENT OF NEW ZEALAND KIWIFRUIT TO AMERICA IN 1964.

would be most complementary to the greens and yellows of fresh produce. The truth is, however, that when my mom decided to launch her business in April 1962, she had about ten days to get everything in order, including a sign for her new business. So she looked up a sign painter in the phone book and told him what she wanted on the sign. He showed up that Monday morning, and, amazingly, the only color on his truck that day was a pale lavender. So, our first sign was purple, and throughout the years we've had purple forklifts, purple carpeting and even purple glazed doughnuts for our company anniversaries! If you visit our facility today, you will see purple flowers in our landscaping, and I still sign all my letters with purple ink.

So now you know why "purple." And how could I forget to include the kiwifruit? My mother is credited with introducing the kiwifruit to America in 1962. She began selling them first as Chinese Gooseberries. The name was a bit confusing, so she changed the name to "kiwifruit" (after the brown, flightless national bird of New Zealand, the kiwi), and the rest is marketing history!

And how did *The Purple Kiwi Cookbook* come about? One of my first jobs at Frieda's, Inc. was to fulfill consumer recipe requests. My mom had some extra space on a package, so she offered free recipes (for Sunchokes® and macadamia nuts). She never expected so many consumers to write in for recipes. But write they did! Over 15,000 letters a year! I still read every letter and e-mail. They're a great source of information.

As the amount and varieties of our produce grew and expanded, so did the requests for recipes. I used to create the recipes in my own kitchen, but eventually we began working with a home economist who helped us create over 850 recipes in our company test kitchen. This cookbook is a collection of over 100 of our favorites.

I'm sure it will come as no surprise that I was the family cook (Mom clearly didn't have time), so it just seemed natural to share some of our favorite recipes. And after ten years of consumers suggesting a cookbook, we finally did it.

When writing a book, there are so many people whom you want to thank and acknowledge. Of course, I

FRIEDA CAPLAN, 1975

want to thank my mom, Frieda, for *not* knowing how to cook. And for being an incredible role model and mentor. And to my sister and business partner, Jackie, thanks for letting me be the "visionary" one . . . while you take care of all the projects I dream up. And thank you to the late Sybil Henderson, who taught me so much about food and the importance of "tasting everything," no matter what it looks like. And to Tristan Millar, who made the production of this book possible—thank you for your energy!

KAREN, FRIEDA, JACKIE, 1985

Our company was the first woman-owned produce company in the U.S., and we're now second-generation. Everything we do is with personal care and affection. Even our products carry a 100-percent satisfaction guarantee. This book is my personal offering to you. I guarantee you will enjoy the recipes as much as my family and the team at Frieda's has!

Enjoy!

Karen

Karen Caplan
President, Frieda's®, Inc.

KAREN, FRIEDA, JACKIE, 1997

TABLE OF CONTENTS

FROM ASIAN PEARS

ASIAN PEARS

BABY BROCCOLI

BABY KIWIFRUIT

BABY SQUASH

BELGIAN ENDIVE

CACTUS PADS

CACTUS PEARS

TO DONUT® PEACHES

CELERY ROOT

CHERIMOYA

CHINESE LONG BEANS

CHIPOTLE CHILES

CILANTRO

CIPOLLINE ONIONS

DAIKON

DONUT® PEACHES

Five-Spice Asian Pear and Jicama Salad

2   cups shredded lettuce
2   cups julienne-cut jicama
2   Asian pears, cored and chopped
1/2 cup golden raisins
     Apple Cider Cream Dressing

Combine the lettuce, jicama, Asian pears and raisins in a medium bowl. Toss gently to mix. Drizzle the dressing over the salad and toss to coat. Serve immediately.
Makes 6 to 8 side-dish servings.

Apple Cider Cream Dressing

1/4 *cup mayonnaise or mayonnaise-style
     salad dressing*
1/4 *cup apple cider or juice*
1/4 *teaspoon Chinese five-spice powder or ground
     allspice*

Whisk the mayonnaise, apple cider and five-spice powder in a bowl until well mixed.
Makes about 1/2 cup.

ASIAN PEARS

Frieda's® coined the name for this Chinese (or Japanese) pear. With the crunch of an apple and the juice of a pear, the Asian pear is loved by kids as an out-of-hand snack. Brown-skinned Asian pears have wine-flavored overtones and make an excellent accompaniment to spicy meat and fish entrées. Originally grown in Japan, and other Asian countries, Asian pears are now grown in California, Japan, Korea and China.

ASIAN PEARS

Lemon Parsley Asian Pear and Shrimp Salad

Lettuce leaves
1   pound cooked large shrimp, shelled and deveined
2   Asian pears, cored and thinly sliced
1   cup julienne cucumber
1   cup fresh watercress
     Lemon Parsley Dressing

Line a large salad platter with lettuce leaves. Mound the shrimp in the center of the lettuce. Arrange the Asian pear slices in fanned groups around the edge of the platter. Place cucumber sticks between Asian pear slices. Top with the watercress sprigs. Blend or shake the dressing before pouring over the salad or serve alongside the salad. *Makes 4 main-dish or 8 first-course servings.*

Lemon Parsley Dressing

$1/2$ cup olive oil or vegetable oil
$1/3$ cup lemon juice
2   tablespoons minced parsley
1   teaspoon sugar
$1/2$ teaspoon salt
$1/4$ teaspoon pepper

Combine the olive oil, lemon juice, parsley, sugar, salt and pepper in a blender container or jar with a tight-fitting lid. Cover and blend until mixed. *Makes about 1 cup.*

Baby Broccoli with Three-Cheese Sauce

1	tablespoon butter or margarine
1	tablespoon all-purpose flour
$1/4$	teaspoon Worcestershire sauce
	Dash pepper
$3/4$	cup milk
$1/4$	cup grated Parmesan or Romano cheese
$1/4$	cup shredded mozzarella cheese
$1/4$	cup shredded sharp Cheddar cheese
1	pound baby broccoli

Melt the butter in a medium saucepan. Stir in flour, Worcestershire and pepper until mixture is blended. Cook until it begins to brown. Stir in milk all at once. Cook over medium heat until mixture thickens and bubbles, stirring constantly. Stir in the cheeses and cook until they are melted. Remove from the heat. Cover and keep warm.

Fill a medium skillet or Dutch oven with water to a depth of 2 inches. Bring to a boil. Wash the broccoli and trim off $1/2$ inch from bottom stems. Place whole stems of baby broccoli in simmering water. Cook for 7 to 9 minutes, or until stems are crisp-tender. Drain well. Arrange the baby broccoli on a serving platter. Stir the sauce and pour over the baby broccoli. Serve immediately.
Makes 4 or 5 servings.

BABY BROCCOLI

Is it a broccoli? Is it a kale? It's both! Baby Broccoli (also called Asparation™ and Broccolini™) is a hybrid crossing of gai lon, a type of Chinese kale, and broccoli. Imagine an asparagus-type stalk topped with delicate dark green florets, more tender and less bitter than broccoli.

Baby Broccoli Rotini

6	ounces ($2^1/3$ cups) uncooked rotini, rigatoni, bowtie or penne pasta
	Salt to taste
1	pound baby broccoli
2	cups chicken or vegetable broth
$1/2$	cup ricotta cheese
$1/4$	cup grated Parmesan or Romano cheese
2	tablespoons olive or vegetable oil
2	garlic cloves, minced
$1/4$	cup dry white wine or chicken broth
1	tablespoon chopped fresh basil
2	teaspoons chopped fresh savory or dill
	Pepper to taste
	Additional grated Parmesan cheese

Cook the pasta in a large pot of boiling salted water according to package directions. Trim the leaves and $1/2$ inch from bottom stems of baby broccoli. Cut the baby broccoli into 1-inch pieces. Combine with the chicken broth in a 2-quart saucepan. Bring to a boil. Reduce heat and simmer, uncovered, for about 4 minutes or until almost tender. Drain, reserving $1/4$ cup of the broth.

Stir together the ricotta cheese, Parmesan cheese and reserved chicken broth in a medium bowl. Set aside. Drain the pasta, but do not rinse. Place in a bowl.

Heat the oil in the pasta pot. Sauté the garlic for 2 minutes. Stir in the wine. Add the ricotta cheese mixture, basil and savory and mix well. Add the broccoli and pasta to the pot and toss to coat with the sauce. Cook, covered, for 1 to 2 minutes or until heated through. Season with salt and pepper. Serve topped with additional grated Parmesan.
Makes 4 servings.

Rainbow Fruit and Endive Salad

3   to 4 Belgian endives
1   Sunrise papaya or $1/2$ Mexican papaya,
     peeled, seeded, and thinly sliced crosswise
6   to 8 baby kiwifruit, stems removed,
     thinly sliced (or 3 to 4 regular size)
1   (11-ounce) can mandarin oranges, drained
1   cup seedless green or red grapes, halved
1   tablespoon pomegranate seeds, or $1/4$ cup
     walnut halves
1   (6-ounce) container orange yogurt
2   tablespoons milk
$1/8$ teaspoon ground allspice or cinnamon

Cut off $1/2$ inch from the base of the Belgian endives and separate the leaves. Arrange the leaves on 4 or 5 individual salad plates. Arrange the papaya and kiwifruit on top. Top with the mandarin oranges, grapes and pomegranate seeds or walnut halves. (At this point salad may be covered and chilled until serving time).

Stir together the yogurt, milk and allspice in a small bowl. Serve with the salads. *Makes 4 or 5 servings.*

BABY KIWIFRUIT

My mother has been dubbed the "Queen of Kiwi," as she imported kiwifruit to the states in 1962 and gave them their modern name (they were formerly called Chinese gooseberry). Kiwifruit have more Vitamin C than most citrus and are a natural tenderizer (use them with meat or veggies, but not in gelatin). Regular kiwifruit will last for almost 6 months in your fridge if you can keep them close to freezing temperature and away from apples and pears. Baby kiwifruit is entirely edible and is sweet and juicy.

Grilled Chicken Salad with Baby Kiwifruit

THERE IS NO NEED TO PEEL BABY KIWIFRUIT. IF THEY ARE OUT OF SEASON, TRY REGULAR KIWIFRUIT, PEELED AND CUT INTO EIGHTHS.

4   (about $1^1/4$ pounds) skinless, boneless chicken
     breast halves
     Olive or vegetable oil
     Salt and pepper to taste
7   to 8 cups baby mesclun mix or mixed
     torn lettuce
6   to 8 baby kiwifruit, stems removed (or 3 to
     4 regular size)
1   cup sliced red onion
1   cup toasted pecan or walnut halves
     Blue Cheese Vinaigrette

Brush chicken breasts lightly with olive oil; season with salt and pepper. Grill over hot coals for 12 to 15 minutes, turning once and brushing with oil, until chicken is no longer pink in the center. Cut the chicken into thin slices.

Combine the mesclun mix, whole unpeeled baby kiwifruit, red onion and pecans in a large bowl and toss gently. Drizzle half the dressing over the salad. Toss well to coat. Spoon onto 4 dinner plates. Arrange sliced chicken over each salad. Drizzle with remaining dressing.
Makes 4 servings.

Blue Cheese Vinaigrette

$1/2$ cup olive or vegetable oil
$1/2$ cup cider vinegar
$1/2$ cup (2 ounces) crumbled blue cheese
1   large shallot, minced
1   tablespoon minced parsley
$1/2$ teaspoon salt
$1/4$ teaspoon pepper

Combine the ingredients in a jar with a tight-fitting lid. Cover and shake vigorously.
Makes about $1^1/2$ cups.

Grilled Baby Squash with Garlic Marinade

ADD THESE SKEWERS TO THE GRILL OR BROILER WITH YOUR ENTRÉE. TO MAKE THE SKEWERS EASIER TO HANDLE, ARRANGE THEM ON A GRILLING TRAY.

16 medium mushrooms
8 ounces baby squash, trimmed
$1/3$ cup olive or vegetable oil
$1/3$ cup white wine vinegar
1 tablespoon chopped fresh basil, dill, chives, chervil, sage or savory
2 garlic cloves, minced
$1/4$ teaspoon salt
$1/4$ teaspoon black peppercorns
4 cherry tomatoes
   Grated Parmesan or Romano cheese and fresh herbs

Trim $1/4$ inch from the stems of the mushrooms. Arrange the squash and mushrooms in a shallow non-metal bowl.

Whisk together the olive oil, vinegar, herbs, garlic, salt and peppercorns in a small bowl. Pour over vegetables. Refrigerate, covered, for 1 to 4 hours.

Drain and reserve the marinade. Thread the mushrooms and squash onto 4 metal barbecue skewers. Grill over medium-hot coals for 7 to 10 minutes, turning once and brushing several times with the reserved marinade, until the squash are crisp-tender. (Or arrange the skewers on a broiler pan and broil 4 inches from the heat for 8 to 10 minutes, turning once and brushing several times with the reserved marinade, until the squash is crisp-tender.)

Arrange the skewers on a serving platter. Thread a cherry tomato onto the end of each skewer. Sprinkle with grated Parmesan and additional chopped herbs, if desired.
Makes 4 servings.

Baby Squash and Goat Cheese Salad

Red Wine Vinaigrette
1 tablespoon olive or vegetable oil
1 pound baby squash, trimmed and halved if large
4 to 5 cups torn mixed salad greens
1 cup garlic croutons
3 ounces goat cheese

Heat 1 tablespoon of the dressing and the olive oil in a skillet. Sauté the squash over medium-high heat for 5 minutes or until tender, stirring frequently.

Combine the squash, mixed greens and croutons in a large bowl and toss gently. Tear the goat cheese into small pieces and sprinkle over the salad. Drizzle the dressing over the salad and toss to coat.
Makes 4 servings.

Red Wine Vinaigrette

$1/4$ cup red wine vinegar
$1/4$ cup olive or vegetable oil
2 teaspoons minced fresh chives
1 teaspoon minced fresh sage or tarragon
1 garlic clove, minced
$1/2$ teaspoon salt
$1/4$ teaspoon pepper

Combine all the ingredients in a jar with a tight-fitting lid. Shake vigorously.
Makes about $1/2$ cup.

BABY SQUASH

Baby squash are special varieties of soft shelled squash grown to be miniatures of summer squash. Baby yellow sunburst, green and gold zucchini, pattypan (summer) and yellow crookneck are elegant and require only brief cooking.

Snap and Crisp Endive Appetizers

BELGIAN ENDIVE LEAVES MAKE THE PERFECT FINGER FOOD. IDEAL FOR PARTIES OR TO TAKE ALONG FOR POTLUCKS.

2   *heads Belgian endive*
9   *ounces Sugar Snap® peas*
4   *ounces soft herb-flavored cheese*
4   *ounces cream cheese, softened*
1   *tablespoon Dijon mustard*
      Fresh herb sprigs, such as dill or watercress

Cut off ½ inch from the base of the endives. Separate the leaves and arrange them on a serving platter. Cut a thin slice from the underside so leaves will sit securely. Remove any strings from the Sugar Snap® peas.

Combine the herb-flavored cheese, cream cheese and mustard in a blender container or food processor. Process until well combined. Pipe or spoon the mixture into the endive leaves. Press one Sugar Snap pod into the cheese mixture in each leaf. Garnish each appetizer with an herb sprig. *Makes 36 appetizers.*

Photograph for this recipe is on page 103.

Belgian-Style Endive

2   *to 4 heads Belgian endive*
2   *tablespoons lemon juice*
2   *tablespoons butter, melted*
½   *teaspoon salt*
½   *cup hot chicken broth*

Place whole Belgian endives in a buttered baking dish. Combine the lemon juice, butter, salt and chicken broth in a small bowl and mix well. Pour over the endives.

Bake, covered, at 350 degrees for 45 minutes to an hour or until endives are tender and golden brown. *Makes 2 servings.*

BELGIAN ENDIVE

Say it EN-dive or on-DEEVE, this cousin of the sunflower is grown without light (and should be stored that way so it does not become too bitter). Look for Belgian endive tips that are light yellow, not green. Store in a brown paper bag in refrigerator. Originally grown in Europe, endive is also grown in the Western U.S. In fact, one of my former classmates from UC Davis is an endive grower in Northern California. Although endive is served largely as a braised vegetable in Europe, Americans enjoy the crunch and bite of raw endive.

BELGIAN ENDIVE

Southwestern Corn and Cactus Chowder

RICH AND HEARTY, THIS SOUP NEEDS ONLY A GOOD CORNBREAD AND A SIMPLE SALAD TO ACCOMPANY IT. FRESH THYME USED IN THIS SOUP LOOKS LIKE TINY STARS.

4   slices bacon
1   cup chopped yellow onion
1   garlic clove, minced
1/2 cup chopped celery
2   cactus pads, eyes trimmed, chopped
2   cups chicken broth
2   cups fresh or frozen corn kernels
     (3 to 4 fresh ears)
1/4 cup chopped parsley
1   tablespoon chopped fresh basil, or
     1 teaspoon dried basil
1   tablespoon chopped fresh thyme, or
     1 teaspoon dried thyme
1/2 teaspoon Worcestershire sauce
1/4 teaspoon white pepper
1/4 teaspoon salt
1/8 teaspoon hot red pepper sauce
2   cups milk or light cream
2   tablespoons all-purpose flour

Fry the bacon in a Dutch oven until crisp. Drain all but 1 tablespoon of the drippings. Crumble the bacon and set aside. Sauté the onion, garlic, celery and cactus pads for 5 minutes or until tender. Stir in the broth, corn, parsley, herbs, Worcestershire, pepper, salt and pepper sauce. Bring to a boil. Reduce the heat to low and simmer, covered, for 10 minutes.

Combine the milk and flour in a small bowl and mix well. Stir into the soup with the bacon. Cook for 5 minutes longer or until thickened, stirring constantly. Taste for seasoning. *Makes 4 to 6 servings.*

Eggs Nopales

1   *cactus pad*
2   *tablespoons butter*
3   *eggs*
     Salt and pepper to taste
½   *cup shredded Monterey Jack cheese*

Cut out the eyes of the cactus pad. Cut the pad into ½-inch cubes. Cover with water in a saucepan. Boil for 10 minutes or until tender. Drain.

    Melt the butter in a skillet or sauté pan. Beat the eggs lightly in a bowl. Stir in salt and pepper to taste. Pour into the pan. Cook until set. Flip the omelette and sprinkle with the cheese and the cooked cactus pad. Fold the omelet in half. Cook until the cheese is melted. Serve immediately.
Makes 1 to 2 servings.

CACTUS PADS

Cactus pads (also called nopales) are the "petals" of the nopal cactus and are an important ingredient in Central and Latin American cooking. Before using cactus pads, use a sharp potato peeler to remove all the prickles (be careful; they are sometimes invisible). With a taste that melds green beans with green pepper, the classic cactus pad dish is scrambled eggs and nopales, served during Lent in Mexico. Some health authorities say that cactus pads may benefit people who are hypoglycemic.

Southwestern Chicken Salad

**GRILLING OR BROILING THE CHICKEN WILL ADD
EVEN MORE FLAVOR.**

4   cactus pears
4   chicken breast halves, cooked
1   cup julienne strips cactus pads, thorns
       removed, blanched
$^1/_2$ cup sliced red onion
$^1/_2$ cup grapes, cut into halves
       Orange Cilantro Dressing
       Lettuce leaves

Hold the cactus pears with tongs. Cut the pears into halves. Scoop out the pulp and chop it. Skin and debone the chicken. Cut chicken into julienne strips. Combine the cactus pear pulp, chicken, cactus pads, onion and grapes in a large bowl and mix well. Drizzle with the dressing and toss gently to coat. Line a platter with lettuce leaves. Spoon the salad onto the lettuce. *Makes 4 servings.*

Orange Cilantro Dressing

$1^1/_2$ tablespoons olive oil
$^1/_4$ cup orange juice
2   tablespoons fresh cilantro, chopped
1   garlic clove, minced
       Pepper to taste

Combine the oil, juice, cilantro, garlic and pepper in a bowl and stir until blended.
(Or you may combine the ingredients in a jar with a tight-fitting lid and shake vigorously.)
Makes about $^1/_3$ cup.

CACTUS PEARS

Razzle-Dazzle Cactus Pear Sauce

MADE WITH RED CACTUS PEARS, THIS SAUCE LOOKS DAZZLING! SERVE IT OVER WAFFLES, PANCAKES, CAKE, ICE CREAM OR FRESH BERRIES.

1/4 cup sugar
3   tablespoons cornstarch
    Dash of salt
6   cactus pears
1/2 cup water
2   tablespoons lemon or lime juice

Mix the sugar, cornstarch and salt in a medium saucepan. Hold each cactus pear with tongs or a fork and cut into quarters. Scoop out the pulp, discarding the skins. Chop the fruit. Purée the fruit in a blender or food processor; strain out the seeds if desired. Stir into the cornstarch mixture along with the water and lemon juice.

Cook over medium-low heat until the mixture boils, stirring constantly. Reduce the heat to low and simmer for 2 minutes or until thickened and clear. Cool slightly. Serve warm or chilled. Store, covered, in the refrigerator for up to 1 week.
Makes 2 cups sauce.

TIP: Use the red, green or orange variety cactus pear, but do not mix colors to keep sauce uniform in color. It's not absolutely necessary to strain the seeds from the cactus pear pulp. They're crunchy but edible.

Jiggly Cactus Pear Salad

SERVE AS A SIDE DISH OR A MAKE-AHEAD DESSERT.

1   (3-ounce) package strawberry gelatin
1 1/2 cups boiling water
3   ounces cream cheese, softened
1/2 cup strawberry low-fat yogurt
3   cactus pears (any variety), peeled and diced

Dissolve the gelatin in the boiling water in a bowl. Cool to room temperature. Beat the cream cheese and yogurt in a medium bowl until blended. Stir in the gelatin mixture and mix well. Chill until the mixture is the consistency of unbeaten egg whites. Gently fold in the cactus pears. Spoon into a 4-cup mold. Refrigerate until firm.
Makes 6 to 8 servings.

CACTUS PEARS

The 300 varieties of cactus pear (also called prickly pear, tuna, or Indian pear) grow almost exclusively in northwest Mexico. The interior of a cactus pear can range from pale yellow to gold to green to red to a deep purple and is thought to be a digestive aid. Several years ago, the "Frieda" variety was developed by a Mexican breeder. This purplish cactus pear was developed in recognition for the pioneering work we'd done in educating the consumer about this sweet, crunchy, watermelon-tasting fruit with edible seeds.

Celery Root, Green Bean and Roasted Red Pepper Salad

2   cups (about 1 large root) peeled julienne-cut
     celery root
2   tablespoons lemon juice
1½   cups haricots verts, or fresh green beans,
     cut into 1-inch lengths
     Salt to taste
½   cup jarred roasted red pepper, well-drained
     and cut into julienne strips
     Lettuce leaves
     Tarragon Mayonnaise

Place the celery root in a bowl of water to
cover. Stir in the lemon juice to prevent
discoloration. Cook the green beans in
boiling salted water for 3 minutes or just
until crisp-tender; drain. Drain the
celery root.

Combine the celery root, green beans
and roasted red pepper in a large bowl and
mix well. You may prepare this salad ahead
to this point and refrigerate, covered, for
up to 24 hours before serving. Line 4 salad
plates or a serving platter with lettuce leaves.

Toss the salad with the Tarragon
Mayonnaise to coat. Spoon the salad onto
the lettuce-lined plates. *Makes 4 servings.*

Tarragon Mayonnaise

¼   cup mayonnaise or mayonnaise-style
     salad dressing
1   teaspoon minced fresh tarragon
1   teaspoon lemon juice
½   teaspoon salt
¼   teaspoon pepper

Combine the mayonnaise, tarragon, lemon
juice, salt and pepper in a bowl and mix
well. *Makes about ¼ cup.*

Warm Celery Root with Mustard Sauce

1   large small celery root (or 2 to 3 small)
2   tablespoons lemon juice
2   tablespoons mayonnaise
2   tablespoons plain yogurt
2   teaspoons Dijon mustard
     Salt and pepper to taste
2   tablespoons minced fresh parsley

Peel the skin off the celery root and cut into
julienne sticks to make about 2 cups. Cover
with water and lemon juice in a saucepan.
Bring the mixture to a boil. Reduce the heat
to low and simmer for 12 to 15 minutes or
until tender; drain.

Stir together the mayonnaise, yogurt,
mustard, salt, pepper and parsley in a
small bowl. Pour the yogurt mixture over
the celery root. Cook for 1 minute, stirring
constantly. Serve warm or chilled.
Makes 3 or 4 servings.

CELERY ROOT

**Your grandmother would not have
known what to do with this so-ugly-
only-a-mother-could-love-it scruffy
sphere. A special plant grown for its
root, celery root, also called celeriac,
has a strong celery flavor and aroma.
Peeled and sliced raw into salads, it
adds a refreshing crunch. Cooked
and puréed, it has a creamy texture
for soups and sauces.**

Cherimoya Avocado Chicken Salad

4   skinless, boneless chicken breast halves, cooked
3   to 4 cups torn lettuce leaves
1   firm, ripe cherimoya (about 1 pound), peeled, seeded and cut into cubes
1   firm, ripe avocado, peeled, pitted and diced
    Lettuce leaves
    Curry Lime Dressing

Cut the chicken into strips. Combine with the lettuce, cherimoya cubes, and avocado in a large bowl and mix well. Spoon onto a platter lined with lettuce leaves. Drizzle the dressing over the salad. *Makes 4 servings.*

Curry Lime Dressing

½   cup vegetable oil
3   tablespoons lime or lemon juice
1   tablespoon light corn syrup
1   green onion, sliced
½   teaspoon curry powder
¼   teaspoon salt

Combine the oil, lime juice, corn syrup, green onion, curry powder and salt in a jar with a tight-fitting lid. Shake vigorously. *Makes about ¾ cup.*

Cherimoya Curaçao

1   papaya
1   firm ripe cherimoya
1   cup fresh pineapple chunks
3   tablespoons curaçao or orange liqueur
    Unsweetened whipped cream
    Grated semisweet chocolate
    Finely shredded orange peel

Cut the papaya into halves lengthwise. Scoop out the seeds. Cut off the peel. Cut the fruit into slices, then cut the slices into halves and place in a medium bowl.

Cut the cherimoya into quarters. Cut out the central fiber and cut off the peel. Cut the quarters into bite-size pieces. Pick out the seeds with the point of the knife. Add to the bowl along with the pineapple. Stir gently to distribute the fruit. Spoon the liqueur over the fruit and toss again. Chill, covered, until serving time. Arrange the fruit on 4 dessert plates. Top with whipped cream, chocolate and orange peel. *Makes 4 servings.*

CHERIMOYA

This creamy, dreamy treasure of a fruit has the texture of shimmery sherbet and a flavor that combines banana, papaya and pineapple. This fruit, also called custard apple, is so wonderful that Mark Twain declared it "deliciousness itself," and Chile has declared it the national fruit. Serve it as they do in Chile, cut in large slices or wedges with a squeeze of orange juice. I have a special affection for cherimoya, as I did my marketing thesis at UC Davis on this wonderful fruit.

Mushroom, Sirloin and Chinese Long Bean Stir-Fry

½ cup beef broth
2 tablespoons oyster sauce
1 tablespoon soy sauce
1 tablespoon dry cooking sherry
1 teaspoon cornstarch
1 or 2 teaspoons olive or vegetable oil
1 pound beef sirloin steak, cut into bite-size strips, trimmed of fat
3 shallots, peeled and sliced
1 garlic clove, minced
8 ounces Chinese long beans, trimmed, cut on the diagonal into 1-inch pieces
8 ounces mushrooms, sliced
  Hot cooked rice

Combine the beef broth, oyster sauce, soy sauce, sherry and cornstarch in a small bowl and mix well.

Heat 1 teaspoon of the oil in a wok or large skillet over high heat. Stir-fry the beef with the shallots and garlic for about 2 to 3 minutes, or to desired doneness. Remove from the wok. Add another teaspoon of oil if necessary, and stir-fry the beans for 3 minutes. Add the mushrooms and stir-fry for 1 minute longer. Remove from the wok.

Stir the sauce again, then pour into the center of the wok. Cook over medium heat until the sauce thickens and bubbles, stirring constantly. Cook for 1 minute longer. Return the beef mixture, beans and mushrooms to the wok. Toss gently to coat with the sauce. Simmer, covered, for 2 minutes or until heated through. Serve immediately over hot cooked rice. *Makes 4 servings.*

CHINESE LONG BEANS

Chinese long beans, also called yard-long beans, are a close relative of black-eyed peas. Young long beans are used in Asian stir-frys, and mature beans are prized for their seeds. Crunchier than green beans, these 12- to 15-inch-long beans can be cut and used in soups, stews or in any recipe where you'd use green beans. Update that green bean, mushroom soup and French-fried onion casserole with Chinese long beans and cipolline onions.

Chinese Long Bean and Black Radish Stir-Fry with Seafood

1/2 pound medium shrimp, unshelled
1 cup Chinese long beans
1 to 2 tablespoons peanut oil or vegetable oil for stir-frying
1/2 cup sliced fresh water chestnuts or drained, canned water chestnuts or sliced jicama
1 red or green bell pepper, cut into bite-size strips
1/4 cup shredded black radish
2 cups shredded Chinese or napa cabbage
1/4 pound flaked cooked crabmeat (optional)
1/4 cup red wine vinegar
2 tablespoons sesame or peanut oil
2 tablespoons soy sauce
1 tablespoon water
1 garlic clove, minced

Cook the shrimp in boiling water to cover for about 3 minutes or until pink. Shell and devein the shrimp. Rinse in cold water. Trim the ends of the Chinese long beans and cut into 2-inch lengths. Heat the peanut oil in a wok or large skillet over medium-high heat. Add the beans, water chestnuts and bell pepper and stir-fry for 3 minutes. Add the black radish, cabbage, crab and shrimp to the wok and stir-fry for 1 minute. Cover the wok and remove from the heat.

Combine the vinegar, sesame oil, soy sauce, water and garlic in a jar with a tight-fitting lid. Shake vigorously until thoroughly blended. Pour over the shrimp mixture and stir to coat. Serve immediately.
Makes 3 servings.

Smoky Chipotle Pasta

3   ounces dried tomatoes, rehydrated, drained
2   to 3 dried Chipotle chiles, rehydrated, drained
1   tablespoon olive oil or vegetable oil
1   cup slivered zucchini or yellow squash
1   cup slivered red or green bell pepper
1½ cups chicken or beef broth
⅓   cup chopped yellow onion
1   garlic clove, minced
¼   cup chopped fresh cilantro
1   tablespoon chopped fresh oregano
¼   teaspoon pepper
½   cup niblet corn
2   cups (about ¾ pound) cooked sliced beef
    sirloin or chicken breast
8   ounces penne, rigatoni or radiatore, cooked,
    drained
    Cilantro sprigs

Chop the tomatoes and mince the chiles; set aside. Heat the oil in a large skillet and sauté the zucchini and bell pepper for 3 minutes, stirring frequently. Combine half the chicken broth, onion, garlic, half of the tomatoes, chiles, cilantro, oregano and pepper in a blender or food processor. Process until smooth. Add to the skillet with the remaining broth, tomatoes, corn and beef or chicken. Simmer over low heat until hot. Toss with the pasta. Garnish with fresh cilantro sprigs. *Makes 3 servings.*

CHIPOTLE CHILES

Chipotle chiles are dried, smoked jalapeños and are my favorite. Chipotles pack a bit of heat but also have a smoky, meaty flavor that livens up soups, sauces, salsas and veggie dishes. Remove the seeds to reduce the heat (don't touch your eyes after doing this!) but not the flavor.

Chipotle Corn Cakes with Chorizo Topping

FOR AN APPETIZER, DROP THE BATTER BY TEASPOONFULS TO MAKE SMALLER CAKES.

4   dried Chipotle chiles
½   cup all-purpose flour
⅓   cup yellow cornmeal
½   teaspoon baking powder
½   teaspoon salt
¾   cup milk
2   tablespoons melted butter
1   egg
1   cup niblet corn
    Vegetable oil
1   pound chorizo or spicy Italian sausage,
    removed from casings, or Soyrizo™
    (soy substitute)
2   green onions, sliced
    Butter, sour cream and fresh cilantro

Reconstitute the chiles in boiling water, then mince.

Stir together the flour, cornmeal, baking powder and salt in a medium bowl. Whisk together the milk, butter and egg in a small bowl until blended. Stir into the flour mixture along with the corn and half of the minced chiles until thoroughly blended. Heat 1 tablespoon of the oil in a nonstick skillet. Spoon the batter into the skillet to form 3- to 4-inch cakes. Cook over medium-high heat for about 2 minutes per side or until golden brown. Keep the corn cakes warm in a 250-degree oven. Repeat until all the batter is used.

Heat 1 tablespoon oil in another skillet. Cook the sausage with the green onions and the remaining minced chiles for about 5 minutes or until the sausage is cooked through, stirring frequently; drain. To serve, arrange 3 corn cakes on each plate. Spoon on some of the sausage mixture. Serve with butter, sour cream and fresh cilantro. *Makes 3 or 4 servings.*

Chipotle Corn Cakes with Chorizo Topping

CHIPOTLE CHILES

Cilantro-Marinated Pork with Green Rice

$^1/_2$ cup white wine vinegar
$^1/_4$ cup olive or vegetable oil
1 cup chopped fresh cilantro sprigs
1 tablespoon chili powder
2 garlic cloves, minced
$^1/_2$ teaspoon salt
$^1/_4$ teaspoon pepper
1 pound boneless pork, cut into $^1/_2$-inch cubes
1 tablespoon vegetable oil
1 cup sliced yellow onion
1 cup bias-sliced carrots
1 medium green, red or yellow bell pepper, cut into $^1/_2$-inch squares
$^3/_4$ cup chicken or beef broth
1 tablespoon cornstarch
1 medium tomato, cut into wedges
   Salt and pepper to taste
   Green Rice
   Cilantro sprigs for garnish

Combine the vinegar, oil, cilantro, chili powder, garlic, salt and pepper in a blender container and purée. Reserve $^1/_4$ cup of the marinade to be used for sauce.

Place pork cubes in a shallow non-metal bowl or a resealable storage bag. Pour the marinade over the pork and stir to coat. Refrigerate along with the reserved marinade, covered, for 2 to 24 hours, stirring occasionally (or squeezing bag) to distribute marinade.

Drain the pork and discard the marinade. Heat 1 tablespoon oil in a large skillet. Brown the pork with the onion, for about 5 minutes, stirring frequently. Stir in the carrots, bell pepper, $^1/_2$ cup chicken broth and reserved marinade. Cook, covered, for 30 minutes, or until the pork is tender. Stir the cornstarch into $^1/_4$ cup chicken broth. Add to the skillet. Bring the mixture to a simmer. Stir in the tomato, salt and pepper to taste. Cover and cook for 2 minutes longer.

Spoon the rice onto a serving platter. Spoon the pork mixture over the rice. Garnish with cilantro sprigs. *Makes 4 servings.*

Green Rice

$2^1/_4$ cups water
1 cup long-grain rice
$^1/_4$ cup finely chopped cilantro

Bring the water to a boil in a 2-quart saucepan. Add the rice. Reduce the heat to low and simmer, covered, for 20 minutes. Stir in the cilantro. Cover and keep warm. *Makes about 3 cups.*

Chicken Wraps with Cilantro and Avocado

TRY THE FLAVORED TORTILLAS FOR COLORFUL WRAPS. HEAT TORTILLAS BY STACKING THEM, WRAPPING IN PLASTIC WRAP, AND MICROWAVING FOR 30 SECONDS.

3   tablespoons vegetable oil
1½   pounds skinless, boneless chicken breasts,
     cut into 1-inch pieces
3   green onions, thinly sliced
1   garlic clove, minced
1   medium red, yellow or green bell pepper,
     cut into strips
⅓   cup chopped fresh cilantro
2   tablespoons lime juice
½   teaspoon salt
¼   teaspoon pepper
½   cup sour cream
¼   cup minced fresh cilantro
2   teaspoons lime juice
¼   teaspoon salt
4   or 5 (10-inch) burrito-size tortillas, warmed
     if desired
1   medium-ripe avocado, peeled, pitted and
     thinly sliced

Heat the oil in a large skillet over medium-high heat. Stir-fry the chicken with the green onions and garlic for 3 to 4 minutes, or until chicken is lightly browned. Remove the chicken from the skillet. Stir-fry the bell pepper in the oil for 3 minutes. Return the chicken mixture to the skillet, along with the cilantro, lime juice, ½ teaspoon salt and pepper and mix well. Cook, covered, for 2 minutes more. Remove from the heat. Drain in a colander.

Combine the sour cream, cilantro, lime juice and ¼ teaspoon salt in a small bowl and mix well.

Lay a tortilla on a work surface or serving plate. Spoon about ½ cup of the chicken mixture onto center of tortilla. Arrange 3 or 4 avocado slices lengthwise over the filling. Top with a spoonful of the sour cream mixture and spread evenly. Fold the bottom of the tortilla over filling, then fold in one side and overlap with the other. Place seam-side-down on serving plate. Repeat the process with the remaining ingredients. *Makes 4 or 5 wraps.*

CILANTRO

Years ago, Ray Marshall, the chef-owner of Acapulco Restaurants, made me like cilantro. The musty aroma of cilantro, also called fresh coriander, and Chinese or Mexican parsley, had never been my favorite. He mixed it with sour cream and some Mexican seasonings and it was great! I like to add cilantro to oil and vinegar salad dressings with a little bit of lime juice and sugar.

CIPOLLINE ONIONS

Braised Lamb Shanks with Cipolline

CIPOLLINE ONIONS COMPLEMENT THE ROBUST FLAVORS OF LAMB BRAISED IN RED WINE.

8 ounces Cipolline onions
3 tablespoons vegetable oil
3 garlic cloves, minced
2 tablespoons vegetable oil
4 lamb shanks (about 3½ pounds)
  Salt and pepper to taste
1½ cups beef broth or consommé
1 cup dry red wine
2 cups trimmed, peeled baby carrots
1 tablespoon chopped fresh basil
1 tablespoon chopped fresh rosemary
1 tablespoon chopped fresh thyme or savory
  Hot cooked noodles or rice

Peel the onions and cut the larger ones into halves, if desired. Heat 1 tablespoon oil in a Dutch oven or deep ovenproof pan over medium heat. Sauté the Cipolline onions and garlic until golden, stirring frequently. Remove the vegetables from the pan.

Heat 2 tablespoons oil. Season the lamb shanks with salt and pepper. Brown the lamb in the hot oil on all sides; drain.

Return the vegetables to the pan and add the broth, wine, baby carrots, herbs and salt and pepper. Bring to a boil.

Bake, covered, at 375 degrees for 1¾ to 2 hours or until lamb is fork-tender, spooning the sauce over the lamb occasionally. Skim the pan juices.

Serve the lamb and vegetables over noodles or rice, drizzled with some of the pan juices. *Makes 4 servings.*

Honey-Roasted Cipolline

THIS RECIPE IS SO SIMPLE. THE TASTE OF HONEY COMPLEMENTS THE SWEETNESS OF THE CIPOLLINE, AND THEY ARE A PERFECT SIDE DISH WITH ROASTS, GRILLED MEATS, OR POULTRY.

8 ounces Cipolline onions, peeled, trimmed
2 tablespoons butter or margarine
1 tablespoon honey
¼ cup chicken or beef broth

Arrange the onions in a single layer in a shallow baking dish. Melt the butter. Stir in the honey. Drizzle the mixture over the onions. Stir to coat with the butter mixture. Pour the broth into the dish.

Bake, uncovered, at 375 degrees for 35 to 45 minutes, or until tender when pierced, stirring occasionally. Remove the onions from the pan with a slotted spoon. *Makes 4 servings.*

CIPOLLINE ONIONS

These slightly flattened pearls of the onion world are also called Italian pearl onions. They are sweeter than traditional pearl onions with a pleasant crunch. A traditional staple of the Italian kitchen, these white gems were introduced by Frieda's®, Inc. to the United States in 1993. Try honey glazed Cipollines on the grill or in the oven.

Thai Greens Salad with Mint and Lemon

3   cups torn Bibb lettuce, spinach or
    napa cabbage
1   cup finely shredded carrot
1   medium tomato, chopped
1   cup shredded daikon radish
2   green onions, bias-sliced into 1/2-inch pieces
2   tablespoons chopped fresh mint
    Lemon Grass Dressing
    Fresh cilantro sprigs

In a salad bowl toss together lettuce, carrot, tomato, daikon, green onions and mint. Drizzle with the dressing and toss well to coat. Spoon onto salad plates. Garnish with cilantro. *Makes 4 servings.*

Lemon Grass Mint Dressing

1/4 cup vegetable oil
1/4 cup lime juice
1   tablespoon chopped fresh mint
1   tablespoon chopped fresh basil
1   stalk fresh lemon grass, peeled and chopped,
    or 1 teaspoon grated fresh lime or
    lemon peel
1/4 teaspoon chili powder

Combine all ingredients in a jar with a tight-fitting lid. Shake vigorously. Remove lemon grass stalk from the dressing before serving over salad. *Makes about 1/2 cup.*

> TIP: To be edible, lemon grass must be peeled to remove the outer husk. The thin, green, chive-like reed inside can then be peeled and chopped to enjoy. If you use lemon grass as is, add it in strips for flavor.

Tiger Stripe Salad with Carrot and Daikon

3   cups shredded bok choy or romaine lettuce
1   cup shredded daikon radish
1   cup shredded carrot
1/2 cup sprouted beans or chopped walnuts or
    peanuts
    Sesame Cilantro Dressing

Combine the boy choy, daikon, carrot and sprouts in a large bowl and mix well. Pour the dressing over the salad. Toss gently to coat. Serve immediately. *Makes 6 servings.*

Sesame Cilantro Dressing

1/4 cup sesame oil
1/3 cup rice wine vinegar or white vinegar
1   green onion, minced
1   teaspoon sugar
2   tablespoons soy sauce
2   tablespoons chopped fresh cilantro

Combine the sesame oil, rice wine vinegar, green onion, sugar, soy sauce and cilantro in a jar with a tight-fitting lid. Cover and shake vigorously to blend. *Makes about 3/4 cup.*

DAIKON

Daikon (also called Japanese or Chinese radish) looks like a one- to two-foot-long, white-fleshed radish with muscles! Don't let its cool-as-a-cucumber appearance fool you— daikon is spicy. Shred peeled daikon into salads and stir-frys. And here's a clothes-saving tip: raw shredded daikon dabbed onto a silk blouse or shirt will remove stains. (This took years of research!)

Grilled Donuts with Ginger Cream

**IT DOESN'T TAKE LONG TO MAKE THIS DELECTABLE
GRILLED DESSERT–THE PEACHES SHOULD JUST BE HOT
AND GLAZED WHEN DONE.**

*About 6 to 8 medium-ripe Donut® peaches,
peeled*
⅓ *cup butter or margarine, melted*
2   *tablespoons packed brown sugar
Ginger Cream*

Cut the peaches into halves horizontally.
Twist the halves in opposite directions to
separate. Remove the pits. Cut each piece
into halves again. Thread the peach wedges
on 4 or 5 barbecue skewers (leave a little
space between each piece for even cooking).
Stir together the melted butter and brown
sugar in a small bowl. Brush the peaches
liberally with the butter mixture. Arrange
the skewers on a lightly oiled grill tray or
broiler pan.

Grill for 6 to 8 minutes, turning once
and brushing several times with the butter
mixture, until peaches are hot and glazed.
(Or, broil 4 inches from the heat for 6 to
8 minutes.) Serve hot with Ginger Cream.
Makes 4 or 5 servings.

Ginger Cream

8   *ounces soft cream cheese*
2   *tablespoons packed brown sugar*
2   *tablespoons orange juice*
1   *tablespoon minced crystallized ginger*

Beat together the cream cheese, brown
sugar, orange juice and ginger in a small
bowl with an electric mixer at medium speed
until well blended. Chill, covered, until
serving time. *Makes about 1 cup.*

Peachy-Keen Tarts

THESE TARTS ARE A GREAT WAY TO SERVE DONUT® PEACHES, INSTEAD OF EATING THEM OUT OF HAND. THEY LOOK COMPLICATED, BUT THEY START WITH CONVENIENT FROZEN PUFF PASTRY SHEETS. LOOK FOR THE DOUGH IN THE DESSERT SECTION OF YOUR GROCER'S FREEZER.

1   egg white, slightly beaten
1   tablespoon water
$^1/_2$ (17.3-ounce) package frozen puff pastry
       sheets, thawed according to package
       directions
       All-purpose flour, as needed
6   to 7 ripe Donut® peaches, peeled, seeds
       removed and thinly sliced
$^3/_4$ cup apricot preserves
       Toasted Coconut Cream

Beat the egg white and water in a bowl with a fork until well blended. Roll out the pastry sheet to a 10×16-inch rectangle on a lightly floured surface. Cut the dough into quarters. Cut each quarter into halves vertically to make 8 rectangles.

Place one rectangle on a large ungreased baking sheet. Brush the edges of the dough with the egg white mixture. Fold the edges over $^1/_4$ inch on all sides, pressing into dough. Flatten all the edges with the tines of a fork. Arrange a row of sliced peaches overlapping inside each rectangle of dough. Place the tarts 1 inch apart on baking sheet.

Heat the preserves in a small saucepan until melted. Brush liberally over peaches. Bake at 375 degrees for 28 to 30 minutes or until the pastry is puffed and golden brown.

Cool the tarts on a rack. Serve warm or cooled topped with Toasted Coconut Cream. *Makes 8 servings.*

Toasted Coconut Cream

$^1/_2$ cup heavy cream
$^1/_2$ cup toasted shredded coconut
1   teaspoon vanilla extract
       Sugar to taste, if desired

Beat the cream in a medium bowl with an electric mixer set at high speed until thick. Stir in the coconut, vanilla and sugar. *Makes about 1 cup.*

DONUT® PEACHES

Originating in China, this international peach traveled from Java to England and then onto the shores of New York and to Washington State. We first began marketing them in 1986. Donut® peaches make a great conversation piece and are a wonderful snack. We came up with the name since they have the shape of a flattened, round donut. They are big in flavor and juiciness, with a small, freestone pit about the size of a pistachio and white pulp.

FROM EDAMAME

EDAMAME

ELEPHANT GARLIC

FENNEL

FINGERLING POTATOES

FRESH GINGERROOT

GOLDEN NUGGET SQUASH

TO KUMQUATS

HABANERO CHILES

HORSERADISH

JAPANESE EGGPLANT

JICAMA

KIWANO®/HORNED MELONS

KOHLRABI

KUMQUATS

CONTENTS

Summer Edamame Salad with Brown Rice

THE COMBINATION OF DILL AND BALSAMIC VINEGAR GIVES THIS SALAD A REFRESHING TASTE, AND THE EDAMAME GOES PERFECTLY WITH BROWN RICE.

1   (12-ounce) package edamame
3   cups cooked brown rice
1   medium tomato, diced
1   cup diced yellow summer squash or zucchini
2   green onions, sliced
    Balsamic Dill Dressing
    Lettuce leaves (optional)

Split the edamame pods and release the beans into a large bowl. (You should have about 1 cup beans.) Discard the pods. Add the rice, tomato, squash and green onions to the bowl. Pour the dressing over the salad. Toss to coat. Chill the salad, covered, for at least 30 minutes or up to 24 hours to allow the flavors to blend. Serve over lettuce leaves, if desired. *Makes 6 servings.*

Balsamic Dill Dressing

3   tablespoons olive or vegetable oil
2   tablespoons balsamic vinegar
1   tablespoon chopped fresh dill
2   garlic cloves, minced
    Salt and pepper to taste

Combine the oil, vinegar, dill, garlic and salt and pepper in a jar with a tight-fitting lid. Cover and shake vigorously until well blended. *Makes about 1/3 cup.*

Chile-Roasted Edamame

THESE TASTY BEANS, MILDLY SPICED WITH CHILE POWDER, WILL GO FAST! YOU MAY WANT TO MAKE SEVERAL BATCHES.

1   (12-ounce) package edamame
2   teaspoons olive or vegetable oil
1/4 teaspoon dried basil, crushed
1/2 teaspoon chile powder
1/4 teaspoon each onion salt and ground cumin
1/8 teaspoon each paprika and black pepper

Split the edamame pods and release the beans into a bowl. Discard the pods. Stir together the oil, basil, chile powder, onion salt, cumin, paprika and black pepper in a small bowl. Drizzle the mixture over the beans and toss to coat. Arrange the beans in a single layer in a shallow baking dish. Roast, uncovered, at 375 degrees for 12 to 15 minutes, stirring once, until the beans begin to brown. Serve hot as a vegetable side dish or cooled as a snack. Refrigerate any leftovers. *Makes 2 or 3 servings.*

EDAMAME

Say "ed-duh-MA-meh" and you'll fit right in at the sushi bar, where edamame is served for snacking, rather than chips. We sell these fresh soybeans in the pod and depodded (the pods are edible but pretty fibrous), ready to eat, so just pop open the package, pop them out of the pod and pop them in your mouth. Soy foods are being recognized as good for you, with natural plant estrogens and other health-related substances. Edamame are addictive with their chewy, crunchy texture.

Elephant (Garlic) Steaks

2   beef or veal steaks or chops
1   tablespoon vegetable oil
3   Elephant garlic cloves, peeled and
     thinly sliced
¼   cup beef broth
⅓   cup dry red wine
1   tablespoon minced fresh parsley
1   teaspoon Worcestershire sauce
½   teaspoon Dijon mustard
¼   teaspoon pepper
2   slices crusty French bread, toasted

Broil the steaks 4 inches from the heat
source, turning once, until cooked to desired
doneness, for 1-inch-thick steaks about
10 minutes total for medium-rare.

Heat the oil in a skillet and sauté the
Elephant garlic for 3 minutes or until almost
tender. Stir in the beef broth, wine, parsley,
Worcestershire sauce, Dijon mustard and
pepper. Bring to a boil, stirring constantly.
Boil for 1 minute. Top the toasted bread with
the steaks. Spoon some of the sauce over
each steak. *Makes 2 servings.*

ELEPHANT GARLIC

**Czech and Yugoslavian immigrants
brought this mild giant to the U.S. in
the 1940s. Elephant garlic looks
gargantuan compared to regular garlic,
but it doesn't pack the garlicky
punch. Actually, it isn't a garlic at all,
but a relative of the leek. I like to
roast unpeeled Elephant garlic whole
until it is soft, squeeze out the
liquified garlic purée, and use it as a
spread or dip for a baguette.**

Garlicky Artichoke Spread

THE MAYONNAISE IN THIS SPREAD GIVES IT A MOUSSE-LIKE TEXTURE. SERVE THIS DELICIOUS MIXTURE WITH WARM FRENCH BREAD, CRACKERS, OR BREADSTICKS FOR DIPPING.

2   *Elephant garlic cloves, peeled and cut into quarters*

1   *(14-ounce) jar marinated artichoke hearts, drained*

$1/2$ *cup reduced-fat mayonnaise*

$3/4$ *cup shredded mozzarella, Monterey Jack or Swiss cheese*

1   *tablespoon minced fresh parsley*

Process the garlic in a food processor or blender until minced. Add the artichoke hearts, mayonnaise and cheese. Cover and blend until finely chopped but not puréed.

Spoon the mixture into a 1-quart baking dish. Bake, covered, at 375 degrees for 25 to 30 minutes, or until heated through. Sprinkle with the parsley. Serve immediately.
Makes about $2^{1}/_{4}$ cups.

TIP: **For a rich, roasted taste, use 2 roasted garlic cloves, peel removed, for this recipe. To roast Elephant garlic, place unpeeled whole garlic bulbs on a greased baking sheet. Bake at 325 degrees for about 1 hour or until very soft. Cool for 5 minutes. Squeeze each clove and the roasted garlic will pop out. Process the soft garlic with other ingredients as directed in the recipe.**

Sautéed Cheese, Fennel and Grape Salad

MELTED THICK SLICES OF MOZZARELLA COMPLEMENT CRISP RAW STICKS OF FENNEL AND JUICY RED GRAPES.

1	fennel bulb
4	cups mixed spring lettuce, torn
1	cup red seedless grapes, cut into halves
8	ounces mozzarella cheese (not fresh mozzarella)
$1/2$	cup Italian-seasoned dry bread crumbs
1	extra-large egg
1	tablespoon water
$1/2$	cup orange juice
$1/3$	cup olive or vegetable oil
2	teaspoons minced fresh chives
	Salt and pepper to taste
2	tablespoons olive or vegetable oil

Trim the leafy end of the fennel bulb to within 1 inch of the head, reserving a few of the leaves. Trim a thin slice from the bottom end of the bulb. Cut the fennel bulb into quarters, then into julienne sticks. Chop 1 tablespoon of the leaves and reserve. Combine the fennel bulb, lettuce and grapes in a large bowl and toss gently.

Cut the mozzarella cheese into eight $1^1/2 \times 1^1/2 \times 1/4$-inch pieces. Place the bread crumbs on a plate. Beat the egg and water in a small bowl with a fork. Dip each cheese slice in egg mixture to coat, then coat with bread crumbs on all sides. Place on a wax-paper-lined tray.

Combine the orange juice, $1/3$ cup olive oil, chives, salt and pepper in a jar with a tight-fitting lid. Shake vigorously.

Toss the salad with the dressing. Spoon onto 4 salad plates. Heat the remaining olive oil in a medium skillet and sauté the cheese for 1 to 2 minutes per side, just until medium brown and melted. Place 2 cheese slices on each salad plate. Sprinkle the reserved fennel leaves over salads. *Makes 4 servings.*

Braised Fennel and Carrots

THE DELICATE FLAVORS OF FENNEL AND CARROTS MARRY WELL IN THIS OVEN-BAKED SIDE DISH. BAKE IT ALONG WITH YOUR ENTRÉE FOR A CAREFREE OVEN DINNER.

2	pounds (2 large bulbs) fennel
$1^1/2$	cups whole peeled baby carrots
1	cup sliced yellow or sweet onion
2	cups vegetable or chicken broth
1	garlic clove, minced
1	bay leaf
$1/2$	teaspoon salt
$1/4$	teaspoon pepper

Trim the leafy end of each fennel bulb to within 1 inch of the head, reserving a few of the leaves. Trim a thin slice from the bottom end of the bulb. Cut the bulb vertically into quarters. Chop 1 tablespoon of the leaves and reserve. Arrange the bulb pieces in a large shallow au gratin or baking dish with the baby carrots and onion. Combine the broth with the garlic, bay leaf, salt and pepper. Pour the mixture over the vegetables.

Bake, covered, at 350 degrees for 50 to 60 minutes, or until vegetables are fork-tender. Discard the bay leaf. Remove the vegetables with a slotted spoon to a serving platter. Sprinkle with fennel leaves. *Makes 6 servings.*

FENNEL

Fennel (also called anise or finocchio) is a multi-layered bulb topped by feathery leaves that resemble dill. Fennel has the mild licorice flavor that food dreams are made of. Whole fennel bulbs can be braised in broth and served with meat or poultry or shaved and used to top breads (fennel-garlic bread, mmm) or garnish soups or vegetables.

Portable Portabello Sandwich

**FOR ADDED FLAVOR, TRY GRILLING THE VEGETABLES
FOR THIS OPEN-FACE SANDWICH.**

1   *medium zucchini*
2   *cups sliced Fingerling potatoes*
2   *large portabello mushroom caps, cut into
    halves horizontally*
1   *to 2 tablespoons olive or vegetable oil*
2   *onion rolls, split, or 4 slices sourdough bread,
    toasted if desired
    Basil Mayonnaise*
4   *slices tomato
    Salt and pepper to taste*
4   *slices provolone, Swiss or mozzarella cheese*

Cut the zucchini into halves crosswise. Cut
each half into slices lengthwise. Arrange the
potato slices and mushroom caps on a broiler
pan. Brush with olive oil. Broil for 5 minutes.
Turn, brush again with oil, and broil for
5 minutes longer. Remove the mushrooms.

Add the zucchini and broil with the
potatoes for 4 to 5 minute, turning zucchini
halfway through the cooking time.

Brush the rolls with basil mayonnaise.
Place a tomato slice onto each roll then
sprinkle with salt and pepper. Arrange the
grilled vegetables on the tomato. Sprinkle
with salt and pepper. Spread with the
remaining mayonnaise. Top each sandwich
with a slice of cheese. Broil until the cheese
melts. *Makes 4 sandwiches.*

Basil Mayonnaise

$^1/_2$ *cup mayonnaise or mayonnaise-style salad
    dressing*
$^1/_2$ *cup fresh basil leaves*
1   *garlic clove, minced*

Combine the mayonnaise, basil and garlic in
a blender container. Process until puréed.
Makes about $^2/_3$ cup.

Garlicky Potatoes Mediterranean

YOU CAN SUBSTITUTE 4 JAPANESE EGGPLANT FOR THE REGULAR EGGPLANT.

12 ounces Fingerling potatoes, cut into
     1½-inch pieces
1   small eggplant, peeled, cut into
     ½×3-inch sticks
2   bell peppers, any color, cut into
     1-inch squares
1   cup sliced red onion
2   tablespoons olive or vegetable oil
2   tablespoons balsamic vinegar
1   tablespoon chopped fresh basil
1   tablespoon chopped fresh oregano
1   tablespoon chopped fresh chives
1   Elephant garlic clove, minced, or
     4 regular garlic cloves
     Salt and pepper to taste

Combine the first 4 ingredients in a large, shallow roasting pan. Whisk together the oil, vinegar, herbs, garlic, salt and pepper in a small bowl until blended. Drizzle the mixture over the vegetables and stir to coat. Roast, uncovered, at 425 degrees for about 20 minutes or until the vegetables are tender, stirring once halfway through the roasting time. *Makes 4 to 6 servings.*

FINGERLING POTATOES

Fingerling potatoes get their name from their appearance, that of a chubby, long finger. I think they taste the way a potato should taste, with lots of flavor and a hint of nuts. Chefs adore the Russian Banana, La Ratte and Ruby Crescent (to name a few) varieties and boil them skin-on or roast them with olive oil and herbs.

Ginger-Stuffed Pork Loin

2½ to 3 pounds boneless rolled pork loin roast
3 tablespoons minced fresh ginger
1 Elephant garlic clove, thinly sliced
1 to 2 tablespoons olive or vegetable oil
1⅓ cups minced onions
2 tablespoons minced fresh cilantro
½ teaspoon salt
¼ teaspoon pepper
1½ pounds baby potatoes, unpeeled
2 bunches baby carrots, trimmed, peeled
   if desired

Cut small slits in the surface of the pork. Insert some of the ginger and garlic into each slit. Rub the pork all over with oil. Place the pork on a rack in a shallow pan. Combine the onions, cilantro, salt and pepper in a small bowl and mix well. Sprinkle over the pork.

Roast, uncovered, at 375 degrees for 2 to 2½ hours until a meat thermometer registers 170 degrees, basting occasionally with pan juices. Remove the pork from the oven. Let stand, covered, for 5 minutes. Remove the strings and carve into thin slices.

Steam the baby potatoes and carrots separately in simmering water until tender, about 7 to 10 minutes for carrots and 12 to 15 minutes for potatoes. Serve with the roast.
Makes 6 to 8 servings.

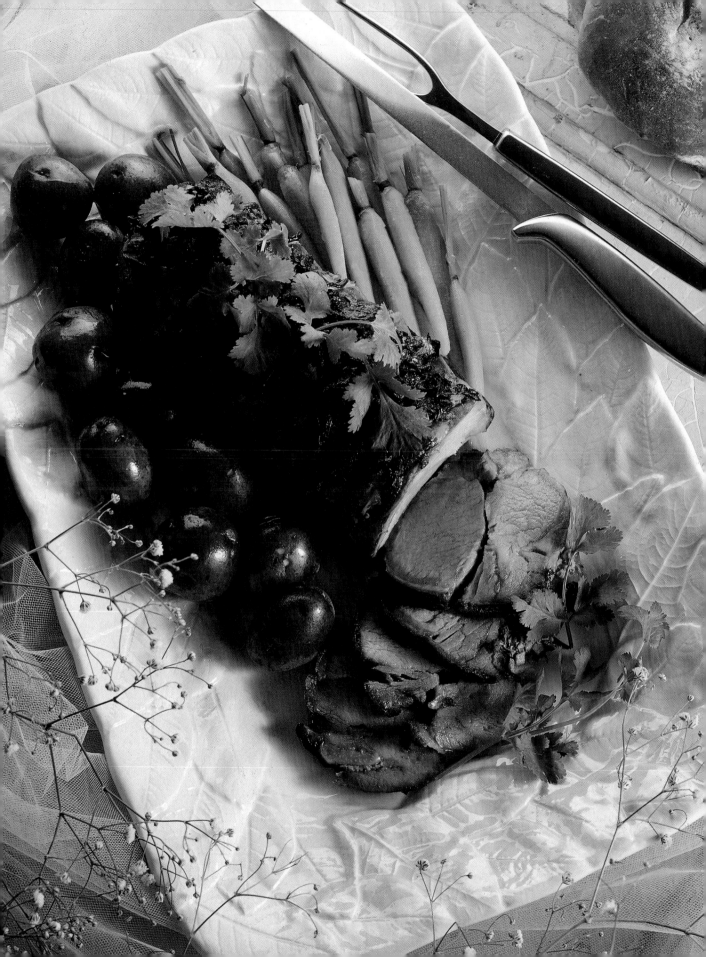

Ginger Sherry Sauce

SERVE THIS EASY SAUCE OVER FISH, CHICKEN, STEAKS, TURKEY, STEAMED VEGGIES, OR ADD A FEW SPOONFULS TO GRAVY OR SALAD DRESSING.

$1/3$ cup dry sherry
$1/3$ cup soy sauce
$1/4$ cup chopped fresh ginger
$1/4$ cup sliced green onions
1   garlic clove, quartered

Combine all the ingredients in a blender or food processor container. Process until finely chopped. Use immediately, or refrigerate in a covered container. *Makes $3/4$ cup.*

Jungle Oatmeal Cookies

$1/2$ cup (1 stick) butter or margarine, softened
$1/4$ cup shortening
$2/3$ cup packed brown sugar
1   egg
1   teaspoon vanilla extract
$3/4$ cup all-purpose flour
$1/2$ teaspoon each baking soda and salt
$1^1/2$ cups rolled oats
1   cup shredded coconut
1   (3-ounce) package dried pineapple chunks, diced dried bananas or diced dried apricots
1   tablespoon minced fresh ginger

Beat the butter, shortening and brown sugar in a bowl with an electric mixer until fluffy. Beat in the egg and vanilla. Stir in the flour, baking soda and salt. Stir in the oats, coconut, pineapple chunks and ginger.

Drop rounded tablespoonfuls of dough 2 inches apart onto ungreased cookie sheets. Bake at 375 degrees for 8 to 10 minutes or until golden brown. Cool the cookies on cookie sheet 2 minutes. Remove and cool completely. Store in an airtight container. *Makes about 20 cookies.*

Gingered Cranberry Sauce

THIS FRUITFUL RELISH IS A WONDERFUL COMPLEMENT TO POULTRY OR PORK OR ON SANDWICHES AS A CONDIMENT.

$1^1/4$ cups apple cider or juice
1   (3-ounce) package dried cranberries
1   cup chopped dried apples or pears
$1/3$ cup raisins
$1^1/2$ teaspoons minced fresh ginger

Combine the cider, dried cranberries, apples, raisins and ginger in a saucepan. Bring to a boil over medium-high heat. Reduce the heat to low. Simmer, covered, for 10 minutes. Remove from heat and let cool. Serve warm or chilled. *Makes 2 cups.*

FRESH GINGER

Throughout the centuries, fresh ginger has been thought to be a cure for many maladies. We know that it's a cure for underflavored soups, rice and vegetable dishes. If you get carsick or seasick, chew on crystallized ginger for relief. Store fresh ginger, wrapped in plastic, in the freezer; just grate what you need and put back in the freezer. Had a rough day? Brew a cup of ginger tea. Just steep several slices of fresh ginger in boiling water for a minute or two.

Golden Nugget Squash with Turkey, Mushroom and Spinach Filling

YOU CAN SUBSTITUTE GROUND LAMB, VEAL, BEEF, OR PORK FOR THE TURKEY IN THIS MAIN-DISH COMBO.

2	Golden Nugget squash, cut into halves
$1/4$	cup water
1	tablespoon vegetable oil
1	pound ground turkey
1	garlic clove, minced
$1/2$	cup minced onion
4	ounces fresh Shiitake mushrooms, stemmed, caps thinly sliced
$1/2$	(10-ounce) package frozen chopped spinach, thawed and drained
1	(16-ounce) can tomato sauce
1	tablespoon chopped fresh basil
1	tablespoon chopped fresh thyme
$1/4$	teaspoon pepper
2	tablespoons grated Parmesan cheese

Arrange the squash halves, cut side down, in a microwaveable dish with $1/4$ cup water. Microwave on High, loosely covered, for 10 to 14 minutes, turning every 3 minutes.

Heat the oil in a skillet. Sauté the turkey, garlic and onion for 3 minutes; drain. Add the mushrooms, spinach, tomato sauce, herbs and pepper to the skillet. Bring to a simmer. Simmer for 5 minutes.

Drain the squash halves and scoop out the seeds. Turn the halves right side up in dish. Fill with the turkey mixture. Sprinkle with Parmesan. Microwave, loosely covered, for 1 minute more or until cheese is melted. *Makes 4 main-dish servings.*

TIP: Just one or two of you for dinner? This recipe can be successfully halved.

Summer Meets Winter Squash with Pesto

4 Golden Nugget, Sweet Dumpling or Sugar Loaf squash
1 to 2 tablespoons vegetable oil
½ cup pine nuts
1 garlic clove, minced
¼ cup sliced green onions
1 cup sliced fresh mushrooms
½ cup diced zucchini
½ cup diced yellow crookneck squash or yellow zucchini
1 cup diced tomatoes
2 teaspoons lemon or lime juice
2 teaspoons chopped fresh oregano, marjoram or sage
2 teaspoons chopped fresh basil
   Salt and pepper to taste
2 tablespoons grated Parmesan cheese

Bake or microwave the Golden Nugget squash until tender (see below). Heat the oil in a large skillet over medium-high heat. Sauté the pine nuts, garlic and green onions for 1 minute. Reduce the heat to medium. Add the mushrooms, zucchini, yellow squash and tomatoes. Sauté for 3 minutes longer or until tender-crisp. Stir in the lemon juice, herbs, salt and pepper.

Scoop the seeds and strings out of the Golden Nugget squash and discard. Place the squash, cut side up, on a platter. Spoon the zucchini mixture into the squash. Sprinkle Parmesan cheese over the top. Sprinkle with additional pine nuts if desired. Serve hot. *Makes 4 servings.*

TIP: To bake squash in the oven, place cut halves or quarters, cut side down, on a baking sheet. Bake at 375 degrees for 35 to 55 minutes or until tender. To microwave squash, place cut halves or quarters, cut side down, in a microwaveable dish with ¼ cup water. Microwave, loosely covered, on High for 5 to 10 minutes, turning once during cooking, until tender. Let stand for 3 minutes.

GOLDEN NUGGET SQUASH

Golden Nugget squash (also called small oriental pumpkin) was our first specialty squash. Golden Nugget looks like a gourd but is actually edible. This squash got our first labels, printed on gold paper to resemble golden nuggets, so we could educate America about the deep orange color and the rich, smooth flavor of the Golden Nugget.

Habanero Chile Chili

THE PERFECT CHILI FOR PARTIES, SUPER BOWL, OR COLD DAYS!
MY ABSOLUTE FAVORITE RECIPE!

3   tablespoons vegetable oil
1   pound lean round steak, cubed
1   cup chopped yellow onion
1   cup chopped red or green bell pepper
2   garlic cloves, minced
1   (16-ounce) can kidney beans
2   cups chopped tomatoes
1   (16-ounce) can low-sodium tomato sauce
1   cup beef broth
1   (11-ounce) package dried blackeyed peas,
    cooked, drained
1   to 2 dried Habanero chiles, rehydrated,
    seeded, minced
2   tablespoons chopped fresh cilantro
1   tablespoon chopped fresh basil
1   tablespoon brown sugar
1   teaspoon Worcestershire sauce
1   bay leaf
1   cup niblet corn, low sodium
    Salt to taste
    Shredded sharp Cheddar cheese
    Warm tortillas

Heat 1 tablespoon oil in a large Dutch oven. Brown the steak in the oil on all sides. Remove from the pan with a slotted spoon. Drain the drippings. Heat 2 tablespoons oil. Sauté the onion, bell pepper and garlic in the oil for 3 minutes. Stir in the beef, undrained kidney beans, tomatoes, tomato sauce, broth, blackeyed peas, Habanero chiles, cilantro, basil, brown sugar, Worcestershire sauce and bay leaf.

Bring the mixture to a boil. Reduce the heat. Simmer, partially covered, for 35 to 45 minutes or until the vegetables are tender. Stir in the corn and salt. Cook for 5 minutes longer. Discard the bay leaf. Ladle the chili into bowls. Top with shredded cheese. Serve with warm tortillas. *Makes 8 servings.*

Jamaican Jerk Chicken

JERK CHICKEN AND OTHER "JERK" MEAT DISHES WERE
SAID TO BE INVENTED BY ESCAPED SLAVES IN JAMAICA, WHO
PRESERVED MEAT BY RUBBING IT WITH A HOT CHILE
PASTE AND THEN GRILLING IT.

1   dried Habanero chile
2   tablespoons prepared yellow mustard
2   tablespoons chopped fresh rosemary
2   tablespoons fresh basil, torn
2   tablespoons chopped fresh thyme
$1/3$ cup chopped green onions
1   garlic clove, cut into quarters
1   teaspoon salt
$1/4$ teaspoon pepper
2   tablespoons lime juice
4   bone-in chicken breasts or leg quarters

Reconstitute the chile with boiling water. Drain, seed and mince the chile. Be sure to wear rubber gloves. Combine the chile with the mustard, rosemary, basil, thyme, green onions, garlic, salt, pepper and lime juice in a food processor or blender container. Process until well blended.

Arrange the chicken in a non-metal dish. Brush $3/4$ of the chile mixture over chicken. Cover the chicken and refrigerate it and the remaining chile mixture for 2 to 6 hours.

Arrange the chicken pieces on a broiler pan or grill. Grill or broil 4 inches from the heat source for 25 to 30 minutes or until juices run clear when chicken is pierced with a knife, turning once and brushing with the remaining chile mixture. *Makes 4 servings.*

Hot! Hot! Hot! Habanero Cheddar Spoon Bread

1   dried Habanero chile
2   cups water
1   cup yellow or white cornmeal
1   teaspoon salt
1   cup cold milk
2   eggs, well beaten
1   tablespoon minced green onions
2   teaspoons baking powder
²/₃ cup shredded Cheddar cheese

Reconstitute the chile with boiling water. Drain, seed and mince the chile. Be sure to wear rubber gloves.

Combine the water, cornmeal and salt in a medium saucepan and mix well. Bring to a boil. Reduce the heat to medium-low and cook for about 5 minutes, stirring constantly (mixture will be thick). Remove from heat. Heat a greased 8-inch baking dish in a 400-degree oven.

Stir the milk into the cornmeal mixture. Stir in the eggs. Stir in the Habanero chile, green onions, baking powder and cheese and mix well. Pour the batter into the hot baking dish. Bake for 30 to 35 minutes or until the center is firm and well-browned. Serve hot with an entrée or salad. *Makes 4 to 6 servings.*

HABANERO CHILES

In the early 1980s, a rocket scientist (really!) with a chile-growing hobby presented us with chiles that were one hundred times hotter than Jalapeños! We had a vision that America was ready for something hot, and Habaneros fit the bill. Caribbean, Thai, and Spanish cuisines get their pungency and heat from the Habanero.

Creamy Horseradish Sauce

²/₃ cup freshly grated horseradish
¹/₃ cup white vinegar
¹/₃ cup mayonnaise
1 tablespoon vegetable oil

Combine the horseradish and vinegar in a blender container. Process at high speed. Add the mayonnaise and blend well. Add the oil and continue blending at high speed until puréed. Refrigerate, covered, until serving time. *Makes 1 cup.*

HORSERADISH

Horseradish makes your eyes tear, it makes your nose run, but it's worth it! This is one ugly veggie; it's knobby and gnarly and usually has a ton of dirt stuck to it. Don't judge a horseradish by its cover! Wash and peel it and add it to sauces. If fresh grated horseradish is a bit too strong for you, use an old Russian culinary trick and grate in some raw beets, whose natural sweetness tempers horseradish's heat.

Horseradish Mashed Potatoes

2 pounds Idaho or russet potatoes, peeled and cut into 2-inch chunks
¹/₃ cup sour cream
¹/₃ cup grated fresh horseradish
2 tablespoons butter, cut up
1 to 1¹/₂ teaspoons salt
¹/₄ cup chopped fresh parsley

Place the potato chunks in a 2-quart saucepan with water to cover. Bring to a boil. Reduce heat and cook for 15 to 20 minutes, or until potatoes are fork-tender. Drain well, leaving potatoes in saucepan.

Combine the sour cream and horseradish in a bowl and mix well. Add the butter to the potatoes, stirring until melted. Add the sour cream mixture. Mash the potatoes with a potato masher or beat with an electric mixer to desired consistency. Stir in the salt and parsley and serve hot. *Makes 5 or 6 servings.*

Sautéed Vegetable Polenta

2   tablespoons olive oil
1/4 cup chopped red onion
1   tablespoon chopped fresh basil
2   teaspoons chopped fresh rosemary
1   garlic clove, minced
1   Japanese eggplant, peeled and chopped
1/3 cup diced yellow or green bell pepper
1/2 cup diced ripe tomato
    Salt and pepper to taste
1   (16-ounce) package prepared polenta
    (original, dried tomato or mushroom flavor)
    Grated Parmesan cheese or shredded
    mozzarella cheese

Heat the oil in a skillet. Sauté the onion, basil, rosemary and garlic for 2 minutes. Stir in the eggplant, bell pepper and tomato. Sauté for 5 minutes or until vegetables are tender, adding a few tablespoons of water if the mixture sticks to the pan. Season with salt and pepper.

Cut the polenta into 1/4-inch-thick circles. Cut the circles into halves. Place on a greased baking sheet. Brush lightly with olive oil. Broil a few inches from the heat for 4 minutes. Spoon some of the vegetable mixture over each piece of polenta. Top with cheese. Broil until the cheese melts. Serve immediately. *Makes about 40 servings.*

TIP: **You can prepare the polenta and the filling up to 2 hours ahead. Let stand, covered, at room temperature until serving time. Then just top with cheese and broil until the cheese is melted and the polenta is heated through.**

JAPANESE EGGPLANT

No, this is not a smooth purple cucumber! Japanese eggplant is slender and a bit sweeter than plump American eggplant and has a purple calyx (the calyx is the hat the eggplant wears). There are many varieties of eggplant including small, round Thai eggplant; Chinese eggplant, which is light purple; Italian, which is plump and purple with a green calyx; baby-sized, white, green, yellow—a full rainbow of colors and sizes.

Multi-Mushroom Pizza

SLICE THIS PIZZA THINLY FOR AN EASY APPETIZER, OR SERVE WITH A BIG TOSSED SALAD AND FRESH FRUIT FOR A VIDEO-NIGHT SUPPER.

1   *(1-ounce) package dried mushrooms (Porcini, Shiitake or Portabello)*
$\frac{1}{2}$ *pound sweet or hot Italian sausage, crumbled*
$\frac{1}{2}$ *cup slivered red, yellow or green bell pepper*
1   *Japanese eggplant, trimmed and sliced thinly crosswise*
$\frac{1}{2}$ *cup sliced red or yellow onion*
2   *cups shredded mozzarella or Monterey Jack cheese*
1   *(12-inch) premade pizza crust*

Reconstitute the mushrooms with boiling water. Drain and slice the mushrooms. Brown the sausage in a large skillet, stirring until crumbly. Remove the sausage with a slotted spoon. Reserve the drippings in the pan.

Sauté the mushrooms, bell pepper, eggplant and onion in the drippings for about 3 to 4 minutes, or until vegetables are tender. Drain well. Sprinkle half or 1 cup of the cheese over the pizza shell. Arrange the sausage and vegetables over the cheese. Sprinkle with the remaining cheese.

Bake at 450 degrees for 8 to 10 minutes or until hot and bubbly. Cut into wedges and serve immediately. *Makes one 12-inch pizza.*

Yucatan Tapenade

SERVE THIS INTRIGUING VEGETABLE MEDLEY AS A GREAT MAKE-AHEAD SIDE DISH.

1   Delicata squash
$1/4$ cup olive oil or vegetable oil
1   garlic clove, minced
$1/2$ cup diced onion
$1/2$ cup diced green bell pepper
1   medium jicama, peeled and chopped
2   cups chopped tomatoes
3   tablespoons white wine vinegar
1   tablespoon lemon juice
1   tablespoon chopped fresh basil or 1 teaspoon
     crushed dried basil
2   teaspoons capers
1   teaspoon salt
$1/4$ teaspoon pepper
$1/8$ teaspoon bottled hot red pepper sauce

Bake the squash in a 350-degree oven for 40 to 50 minutes or until tender. Let cool. Cut the squash into halves lengthwise. Scoop the pulp from the shell and set aside.

Heat the oil in a large skillet. Add the garlic, onion and bell pepper and sauté until tender. Stir in the squash pulp, jicama, tomatoes, vinegar, lemon juice, basil, capers, salt, pepper and hot sauce. Bring the mixture to a boil.

Reduce the heat and simmer, uncovered, for 20 minutes, stirring occasionally. Serve hot or chilled. *Makes 6 servings.*

Corn, Jicama and Pineapple Salsa

HABANERO CHILE IS THE SECRET TO THIS SPUNKY COMBINATION. SPOON OVER ANY STEAMED OR COOKED VEGETABLE, SCRAMBLED EGGS, GRILLED MEATS, POULTRY, OR FISH.

$1^1/_2$ cups finely chopped jicama
1   cup finely chopped fresh pineapple
1   cup niblet corn
$^1/_2$ cup diced green or red bell pepper
1   Habanero chile, finely chopped
2   tablespoons chopped fresh cilantro
1   garlic clove, minced

Combine the jicama, pineapple, corn, bell pepper, Habanero chile, cilantro and garlic in a blender or food processor container. Process in 2 batches, using a few stop-and-start motions, for a relish-like consistency. Cover and chill for at least 1 hour to allow flavors to blend. *Makes $3^1/_2$ cups.*

JICAMA

Can you say "HEEK-a-mah?" Don't be deceived by the brown, papery peel; jicama's interior stays white and crunchy when cooked and is a good replacement for water chestnuts. Jicama, also called yam bean, originated in Mexico and was transported by Spanish explorers to the Philippines, where it became important in Asian cuisine. There are two varieties of jicama: milk and water. The juiciness and starchiness are the difference.

Horned Melon and Lime Mousse

TRY USING THE COLORFUL MELON SHELLS TO SERVE THIS CELESTIAL COMBINATION. IT WILL DAZZLE YOUR TASTE BUDS!

2   Kiwano®/Horned Melons
3   tablespoons lime juice
     Grated peel of 1 lime
$2/3$ cup granulated sugar
1   envelope unflavored gelatin
1   cup whipping cream, whipped
2   egg whites, stiffly beaten
     Few drops green food coloring (optional)
     Lime slices, horned melon slices or fresh mint
     sprigs for garnish

KIWANO®/HORNED MELONS

Imagine a personal-size, bright orange, porcupine-style melon. That's a Kiwano®, also called Horned Melon or jelly melon. The interior has a luscious lime green, banana jelly texture with hints of cool cucumber and lime. Kids love that they're green and slimy. (Thanks, kids!) When Paramount Studios is filming the Star Trek series, their set designers come and shop at our warehouse; one of their favorites is the Horned Melon.

Cut the melons into halves lengthwise. Use a grapefruit knife or small sharp knife to scoop out the pulp. Spoon the pulp into a blender or food processor container. Process until puréed. Strain out and discard the seeds and pulp, reserving the juice. Chill the shells, if desired, to use later for serving containers.

Stir together the melon juice, lime juice, lime peel, sugar, and gelatin in a small saucepan. Let stand for 5 minutes. Then heat over medium heat for about 2 minutes, stirring until the gelatin is dissolved. Remove from the heat. Chill the mixture in the refrigerator for about 30 minutes or until it is partially set; mixture will be the consistency of beaten egg whites.

Fold in the whipped cream, egg whites and food coloring. Spoon into a medium bowl. Chill, covered, for several hours or until firm. Serve in 6 long-stemmed goblets or spoon into reserved melon shells. Garnish with slices of lime and Horned Melon or mint sprigs. *Makes 6 servings.*

Grilled Beef with Horned Melon Sauce

TRY THIS DISH WITH GRILLED LAMB OR PORK INSTEAD OF BEEF.

1   *Kiwano®/Horned Melon*
1   *pound lean beef sirloin, trimmed of all fat*
4   *cups shredded lettuce*
1½ *cups julienne-cut cucumber*
      Horned Melon Sauce

Cut the melon into halves. Cut crosswise into thin slices. Cut off the outside skin. Cut the beef into thin slices. Grill or broil the beef to desired doneness. Arrange the lettuce on a large salad platter. Top with the grilled beef, melon slices and cucumber sticks. Spoon the sauce over the top. *Makes 4 servings.*

Horned Melon Sauce

1   *Kiwano®/Horned Melon*
3   *tablespoons lime juice*
1   *green onion, minced*
1   *teaspoon vegetable oil*
¼   *teaspoon cumin*
1   *garlic clove, minced*

Cut the melon into halves lengthwise. Use a grapefruit knife or small sharp knife to scoop out the pulp. Combine the melon pulp, lime juice, green onion, oil, cumin and garlic in a blender or food processor container. Cover and process until well blended. M*akes about 1¼ cups.*

Indian Kohlrabi Fruit Salad

1   to 2 bulbs purple or green kohlrabi
1½   cups shredded green cabbage
1½   cups shredded red cabbage
½   cup each raisins and chopped dried apricots
     Curry Yogurt Dressing

Cut off and discard the root end and all stems and leaves from the kohlrabi bulbs. Wash and peel the kohlrabi. Cut into ¼-inch cubes. Combine with the cabbages, raisins and apricots in a large bowl and mix well. Top with the dressing. Toss gently to mix. *Makes 6 servings.*

Curry Yogurt Dressing

⅓   cup mayonnaise
⅓   cup plain yogurt
1   tablespoon milk
1   green onion, sliced
2   teaspoons each curry powder and honey

Mix all ingredients in a small bowl. Use immediately or refrigerate, covered, for up to 24 hours. *Makes about ¾ cup.*

KOHLRABI

Let's see, picture a solid pale green (or sometimes purple), smooth bulb, about the size of a small onion. Give it several long, slender stems, the same color as the bulb. There! You have a kohlrabi, also called cabbage turnip! Oh, and if there are leaves attached, they can be cooked just like spinach. The bulb is very firm and tastes like a sweet turnip; peel it and slice it raw into salads.

Kohlrabi Salad Julienne

HERE'S A DELICIOUS AND UNUSUAL SALAD TO TAKE TO YOUR NEXT POTLUCK.

2   bulbs purple or green kohlrabi
⅔   cup Sugar Snap® peas, strings removed
1   cup julienne-sliced summer squash, such as zucchini, yellow zucchini, yellow crookneck or pattypan squash
1   cup julienne-sliced carrots
     Lemon Poppy Seed Dressing

Cut off and discard the root end and all stems and leaves from kohlrabi bulbs. Wash and peel the kohlrabi. Cut into julienne sticks (you should have about 1½ cups). Cut the Sugar Snap® peas into halves crosswise. Combine the kohlrabi, Sugar Snap® peas, squash and carrots in a large bowl and mix well. Toss the salad with dressing to coat. Refrigerate any leftovers. *Makes 4 or 5 servings.*

Lemon Poppy Seed Dressing

3   tablespoons mayonnaise or mayonnaise-style salad dressing
1   tablespoon cider vinegar
1   teaspoon poppy seeds
½   teaspoon honey

Combine the mayonnaise, vinegar, poppy seeds and honey in a small bowl and mix until well combined. Refrigerate, covered, until ready to use. *Makes about ¼ cup.*

Duck and Kumquat Salad

Romaine lettuce leaves
1 Belgian endive, leaves separated
1½ cups chilled julienne-sliced cooked duck or chicken breast
⅔ cup green or red seedless grapes
3 tablespoons chopped walnuts or slivered almonds
Alfalfa sprouts
Kumquat Dressing

Line a large serving platter or individual plates with romaine leaves. Arrange the Belgian endive, duck, grapes and walnuts on the leaves. Garnish with alfalfa sprouts. Serve with the dressing on the side.
Makes 2 servings.

Kumquat Dressing

½ cup red or white wine vinegar
½ cup chopped kumquats
⅓ cup vegetable oil
2 tablespoons honey

Combine the vinegar, kumquats, oil and honey in a blender or food processor container. Process until the kumquats are very finely chopped. Chill until serving time.
Makes 1½ cups.

Kumquat Macadamia Chicken

1 (3-pound) chicken, cut up
2 tablespoons vegetable oil
½ cup dry white wine
½ to 1 cup pineapple juice
1 small onion, thinly sliced, separated into rings
1 to 2 tablespoons minced fresh ginger
½ teaspoon freshly ground black pepper
⅔ cup coarsely chopped macadamia nuts
6 kumquats, thinly sliced
Hot cooked rice

Brown the chicken on all sides in the heated oil in a skillet over high heat. Add the wine, ½ cup of the pineapple juice, onion, ginger and pepper. Simmer, covered, for 30 minutes, adding more pineapple juice to pan if needed. Uncover and add the macadamias and kumquats. Cook for 5 to 10 minutes more or until juices run clear when chicken is pierced with a knife. Mound the rice on a serving platter. Top with chicken, macadamias and kumquats. Spoon some of the sauce over dish. *Makes 6 servings.*

KUMQUATS

Kumquat is the inside-out fruit! The edible peel of the kumquat is sweet and the interior is tart. This miniature football-shaped fruit can be cut into green, poultry, or seafood salads; used as a garnish for sweet desserts, or used in place of lemon slices. I remember eating kumquat skins (I never ate the inside) instead of having orange juice in the mornings. Kumquat fact: Although it resembles miniature citrus, botanists have decided that kumquats belong to their own genus. So there!

KUMQUATS

FROM LEEKS

LEEKS

LEMON GRASS

LYCHEES

MALANGA

MANGO

MANZANO BANANAS

MORO ORANGES

OROBLANCOS

TO PURPLE POTATOES

PASSION FRUIT

PEARL ONIONS

PEPINO MELONS

PLANTAINS

POBLANO CHILES

PURPLE ASPARAGUS

PURPLE POTATOES

Green Leeks Française

SERVE THESE AS A SIDE DISH OR SALAD ON LETTUCE-LINED PLATES.

2 to 3 leeks, well washed
1 to 2 cups chicken broth
¼ cup olive or vegetable oil
3 tablespoons vinegar
1 garlic clove, minced
1 tablespoon chopped fresh dill
   Salt and pepper to taste

Trim off green tops of leeks and discard. Cut the leeks into slices. Combine in a saucepan with enough of the broth to cover. Bring to a boil. Reduce the heat to low and simmer, partially covered, for 3 to 5 minutes or until tender. Drain and place in a non-metal dish. Combine the oil, vinegar, garlic, dill, salt and pepper in a cruet. Cover and shake vigorously. Pour over the leeks. Chill, covered, for 1 to 24 hours. Drain before serving. *Makes 4 servings.*

LEEKS

Known as "poor man's asparagus," leeks are a stalky, mild onion cousin. The green, tough portion of the leaves is used by chefs instead of cheesecloth to tie up sachets for soups and stocks or cut into thin strips and used to wrap "bundles" of matchstick-cut carrots or whole green beans. Look for leeks with lots of white, as that's the edible part. Be sure to strip off the tough outer leaves and rinse well to get all of the sand out.

Leek and Mushroom Tart

1 (9-inch) homemade or deep-dish pastry shell
2 tablespoons butter or margarine
2 cups chopped leeks
1 cup chopped fresh mushrooms
3 eggs
1 cup light cream or milk
1 tablespoon chopped fresh chervil, or
   1 teaspoon crushed dried chervil
1 teaspoon salt
⅛ teaspoon pepper
   Few drops of bottled hot pepper sauce

Bake the pastry shell at 450 degrees for 5 minutes. Meanwhile, melt the butter in a skillet. Sauté the leeks and mushrooms for 5 minutes, or until vegetables are tender.

Beat the eggs, light cream, chervil, salt, pepper and hot sauce in a deep bowl with a wire whisk until well combined. Spoon the leek mixture into the hot pie shell. Place the pie on the oven rack and pour in the egg mixture. Reduce oven temperature to 325 degrees. Bake for about 45 minutes, or until a knife inserted just off-center comes out clean. Let stand for 10 minutes before serving. *Makes 6 servings.*

Light Lemon Hollandaise

3   tablespoons reduced-fat mayonnaise or mayonnaise-style salad dressing
$1/3$ cup lowfat milk
$1/4$ cup plain lowfat yogurt
1   egg yolk, lightly beaten
2   tablespoons minced fresh lemon grass (bulb only)
$1/4$ teaspoon dry mustard
     Dash of cayenne pepper
$1/4$ teaspoon black pepper
     Salt to taste

Process the mayonnaise, milk, yogurt, egg yolk, lemon grass, mustard, cayenne, black pepper and salt in a food processor or blender for 1 minute or until lemon grass pieces are pulverized. Transfer the mixture to a medium saucepan. Cook over medium-low heat for 3 to 5 minutes or until heated through, stirring constantly with a wire whisk. Do not allow the sauce to boil or it will curdle. *Makes 1 cup.*

LEMON GRASS

Mai Pham, Sacramento, California, chef and restaurateur, was so enamored of this herb that she named her restaurant the Lemon Grass. Looking a bit like a stiff, solid, paler version of a green onion, lemon grass adds flavor to stocks, broths, soups, rice and noodle dishes. Thai and Vietnamese chefs use a lot of lemon grass. Cook with the white section of the stem and discard, just like a bay leaf, before serving.

Thai Chicken and Coconut Soup

5   to 6 dried Bird chiles or any small red chile, rehydrated
$3^3/4$ cups skim milk
2   tablespoons unsweetened coconut milk
2   cups reduced-sodium chicken broth
2   pieces lemon grass, peeled and cut into thirds
3   chicken breasts, skinned, boned, and cut into $1/2$-inch pieces
1   tablespoon minced fresh ginger
$1^1/2$ cups half-slices of carrot
1   cup sliced fresh mushrooms
3   green onions, cut into $1/2$-inch pieces
2   tablespoons minced fresh cilantro
1   teaspoon cumin
$1/4$ teaspoon salt
$1/4$ teaspoon pepper
2   tablespoons lime juice
     Fresh cilantro sprigs

Remove the stems and seeds from the chiles and mince. Bring the milk, coconut milk and broth to a boil in a large saucepan. Add the lemon grass, chicken, chiles and ginger. Reduce the heat to low and simmer for 15 minutes.

Strain the soup, reserving the chicken. Remove the lemon grass pieces. Return the strained liquid to the saucepan. Add the chicken, carrot, mushrooms, green onions, cilantro, cumin, salt and pepper.

Bring the soup to a boil; reduce the heat to low. Simmer for 5 minutes or until vegetables are tender. Stir in lime juice. Garnish with fresh cilantro. *Makes 4 servings.*

Lemon Mousse Pudding with Lychees

THIS ETHEREAL PUDDING SEPARATES INTO A DARKER LEMON LAYER AT THE BOTTOM AND A MOUSSE LAYER ON THE TOP.

1   tablespoon butter
1   envelope unflavored gelatin
¼   cup water
3   egg yolks
1   cup sugar
1   teaspoon vanilla extract
⅓   cup lemon juice
     Grated peel of 1 lemon
24   fresh lychees
1   cup whipping cream
     Fresh mint sprigs

Butter 8 individual dessert dishes. Sprinkle the gelatin over the water in a small saucepan. Heat the mixture, stirring until the gelatin is dissolved. Combine the egg yolks, sugar and vanilla in a small, heavy saucepan. Cook over medium heat until the mixture thickens slightly and the sugar is melted, stirring constantly. Do not boil or mixture will curdle.

Stir the gelatin mixture into the egg mixture along with the lemon juice and lemon peel. Refrigerate, covered, for 30 to 45 minutes or until the mixture is the consistency of unbeaten egg whites.

Break off the outer shells of the lychees, peel back and discard. Pull away the white pulp from inside the seed and discard the seed. Reserve 8 lychees for garnish. Beat the cream in a bowl with an electric mixer set at high speed until stiff. Stir half of the cream into the gelatin mixture with a wire whisk until well-blended. Fold the remaining cream into the gelatin mixture with a rubber spatula, until no traces of white remain, then fold in the lychees. Spoon the mixture into the prepared dessert dishes. Chill, covered, along with the remaining lychees, for at least 2 hours or until set. Garnish each mousse with 1 of the reserved lychees and sprigs of mint. *Makes 8 servings.*

Gingered Mandarin Lychees

SERVE THIS COMBINATION AS A SALAD OR DESSERT.

1   pound fresh lychees
1   (11-ounce) can mandarin oranges, drained
2   tablespoons orange juice
2   teaspoons lemon juice
½   teaspoon minced fresh ginger
     Fresh mint sprigs

Break off the outer shells of the lychees, peel back and discard. Pull away the white pulp from inside the seed and discard the seed. Lychee will come off in segments. Put the segments into a bowl. Add the oranges, orange juice, lemon juice and ginger and mix gently but well. Chill, covered, until serving time. Garnish with fresh mint. *Makes 4 or 5 servings.*

LYCHEES

Natural deceptions! Fresh lychees, the size of large marbles, have a prickly-looking red skin. Easily peeled with your hands, lychees have an interior that is paradise on earth. Its cool, juicy, fragrant interior has been likened to peeled grapes and white cherries. Lychees are highly prized in Asian countries, as their season is so fleeting, typically only during the month of June. Nowadays Frieda's® is able to extend the season, obtaining lychees from Florida, Mexico, and Israel.

Malanga, Black Bean and Pepper Salad

MALANGA TAKES THE PLACE OF POTATOES IN THIS COMFORTING SALAD. SERVE IT WARM AND IT WILL REMIND YOU OF A HOT GERMAN POTATO SALAD. OR CHILL THIS SALAD TO SERVE THE NEXT DAY.

1   pound malanga root (about 2 roots),
     peeled, cut into $1/2$-inch pieces
2   cups chicken or beef broth
1   (15-ounce) can black beans, rinsed, drained
1   cup jarred roasted red peppers, drained, cut
     into bite-size strips
     Red Onion Cilantro Dressing

Place malanga pieces in a 2-quart saucepan with broth. Bring to boiling; reduce heat and simmer, partially covered, about 15 minutes or until tender; drain.

In a large bowl, combine the cooked, drained malanga, black beans and roasted red peppers. Pour dressing over salad; toss well to coat. Serve or cover and chill for up to 24 hours before serving.
Makes 4 to 6 servings.

Red Onion Cilantro Dressing

$1/4$ cup olive or vegetable oil
$1/4$ cup lime or lemon juice
$1/4$ cup minced red onion
2   tablespoons chopped fresh cilantro
2   garlic cloves, minced
$1/2$ teaspoon salt
$1/4$ teaspoon crushed red pepper

Combine the oil, lime juice, onion, cilantro, garlic, salt and red pepper in a jar with a tight-fitting lid. Cover and shake vigorously. *Makes about $3/4$ cup.*

Malanga Raisin Pudding

SOMETHING SPECIAL HAPPENS WITH THE COMBINATION OF THESE INGREDIENTS. THIS RECIPE WAS AN INSTANT HIT, AND WE BEGAN SERVING IT TO OUR CLIENTS AT MEETINGS. THE MALANGA TEXTURE IS LIKE A THICKENED BREAD.

12   ounces malanga, peeled, cut into
      $1/2$-inch cubes
4   eggs
$1^1/4$ cups packed brown sugar
$1^1/2$ cups milk
1   teaspoon vanilla extract
$1/2$ cup raisins
      Whipped cream or vanilla yogurt

Combine the malanga chunks and water to cover in a medium saucepan. Bring to a boil. Reduce the heat to low. Simmer, covered, for 20 minutes, or until very tender. Drain and mash. Process the eggs with the brown sugar, milk and vanilla in a blender or food processor until well blended. Add the malanga and process until mixed. Stir in the raisins. Spoon the mixture into an ungreased 7×11-inch baking dish. Bake at 350 degrees for 25 to 30 minutes or until golden. Serve warm or chilled, topped with whipped cream or yogurt. *Makes 6 to 8 servings.*

MALANGA

Malanga, a native of the American tropics, is considered one of the oldest root vegetables in the world. Use as you would a potato or starchy vegetable, and don't be distracted by malanga's shaggy brown exterior. Do note that malanga must be cooked before eating. Get crazy—peel and cube some malanga and bring a malanga salad to the company picnic this year.

Berry Mango Smoothie with Tofu

1   cup chopped fresh mango
1   cup lowfat milk
1   cup fresh or frozen raspberries or strawberries
$1/2$ cup soft tofu, drained and cut up
1   to 2 teaspoons honey
1   teaspoon vanilla extract
6   ice cubes

Combine the mango, milk, raspberries, tofu, honey and vanilla in a blender or food processor container. Process, covered, until smooth. With the machine running, add the ice cubes through the lid or feed tube. Process until finely chopped and well blended. Pour into 2 glasses. Serve immediately.
Makes 2 servings.

MANGO

When I was a little girl, I was enchanted by the aroma of mangos my mother brought home with her. In the early 1960s my mother brought big, green flavorful mangos from Florida to California. Frieda's® has recently discovered Pango™ mangos from Puerto Rico that are so reminiscent of those first juicy mangos. We are thrilled to be distributing them throughout the country.

Floribbean Pizza Dessert

HERE'S A COLORFUL, FESTIVE DESSERT FOR A SPECIAL OCCASION—OR JUST BECAUSE!

1   (20-ounce) roll refrigerated sugar cookie dough
1   (4-ounce) package vanilla instant pudding mix
$1^3/4$ cups milk
1   fresh mango, peeled, seeded and thinly sliced
$1/2$ cup sliced fresh strawberries
1   kiwifruit, peeled, cut into halves and sliced
    Frozen whipped topping
$1/4$ cup toasted shredded coconut

Cut the cookie dough into $1/4$-inch-thick slices. Arrange $3/4$ of the slices in a lightly greased 12-inch pizza pan. Press the dough into the pan to make a crust. Bake at 350 degrees for 12 to 14 minutes or until lightly browned. Cool for 10 minutes while preparing the filling. (Reserve the remaining cookie dough for another use or bake as package directs.)

Stir together the pudding mix and milk until well blended. Spread over the crust. Arrange slices of mango, strawberries and kiwifruit decoratively over filling. (If preparing ahead, cover and chill up to 2 hours before serving.) To serve, spoon dollops of whipped topping over the pizza and sprinkle with toasted coconut. Cut into 8 wedges. You may use a small banana, cut into slices, in place of the kiwifruit.
Makes 8 servings.

Mexican Fruit Salad

THE BROKEN CINNAMON STICKS ADD A SPICY FLAVOR TO THIS COMPOTE. HOWEVER, THEY SHOULD NEVER BE EATEN.

1/2   *cup sugar*
1/2   *cup water*
2   *cinnamon sticks, broken*
3   *ripe Manzano bananas, peeled and cut into 1/2-inch slices*
1   *tablespoon lime juice*
2   *Moro oranges or navel oranges, peeled*
1   *cup pineapple chunks*
1   *medium strawberry papaya or other papaya, peeled, seeded and cut into 1-inch chunks*

Combine the sugar, water and cinnamon sticks in a small heavy saucepan. Bring to a boil over medium heat, stirring to dissolve the sugar. Reduce the heat to low and simmer for 5 minutes. Cool in the refrigerator for about 15 to 20 minutes or until the mixture is close to room temperature.

Combine the banana slices and lime juice in a large bowl and mix well. Cut the oranges into 1/4-inch-thick slices, then cut the slices into halves. Add the oranges, pineapple and papaya to the bowl. Pour the sugar syrup over the fruit and toss gently.

Chill, covered, in the refrigerator for at least 30 minutes to 1 hour before serving to allow flavors to blend. You may leave cinnamon sticks in mixture if desired for garnish (do not eat). *Makes 4 servings.*

Orange-Glazed Bananas

BE CAREFUL NOT TO OVERCOOK THE BANANAS TO PRESERVE THEIR TEXTURE. SERVE THIS AS A BREAKFAST FRUIT COMPOTE, A DESSERT SAUCE OVER ICE CREAM, PUDDING, CAKE, OR OVER WAFFLES OR PANCAKES.

3   *to 4 ripe Manzano bananas, cut into 1/2-inch slices*
1   *tablespoon lemon juice*
2   *tablespoons butter*
1   *tablespoon brown sugar*
2   *to 3 tablespoons fresh orange juice*
     Grated peel of 1 orange

Combine the bananas with the lemon juice in a large bowl and mix well. Melt the butter in a large skillet. Stir in the brown sugar. Stir in the bananas with orange juice and orange peel. Cook the bananas for 2 to 3 minutes or until softened and glazed. *Makes 3 or 4 servings.*

MANZANO BANANAS

There are dozens of banana varieties to sample; be sure to try some Manzanos, also called apple bananas. Manzanos are short and chubby, green when unripe and black at the height of ripeness. Imagine a banana that has some hints of strawberry and apple (Manzano means "apple" in Spanish) and you've imagined a Manzano. Let the skin get dark for the sweetest flavor.

Sunburst Sorbet

THIS SORBET HAS A CREAMY TEXTURE AND THE RICH, SWEET FLAVOR OF MORO ORANGES.

6   medium (about 3 pounds) Moro oranges
$1/2$ cup water
$1^1/3$ cups light corn syrup
1   cup half-and-half
    Dash of salt

Cut the oranges into halves. Cut the pulp segments from the shell and membrane with a small sharp knife. Process the pulp in a blender or food processor until it is puréed. Pour the pulp through a sieve, pressing hard on the solids with the back of a spoon. You should have about 2 cups of juice. Combine the juice with the water, corn syrup, half-and-half and salt and mix well. Freeze the mixture in an ice cream maker according to the manufacturer's directions. *Makes 10 to 12 servings.*

TIP: No ice cream maker? Try this: Pour the orange mixture into a shallow metal pan; freeze until partially frozen. Spoon the mixture into a chilled bowl and beat with an electric mixer until fluffy. Spoon into a freezer container; freeze until firm.

MORO ORANGES

Vibrant and dramatic, the interior of a Moro orange (also called a blood orange) resembles a red rose and tastes like an orange kissed by a raspberry. Used by classical chefs to impart a blush to silky sauces, the Moro orange is sweet, with less acid than juice oranges. I serve fresh Moro orange juice as a beautiful beverage for family brunch and business meals.

Roast Beef and Moro Orange Salad

ORANGES AND ROAST BEEF MAKE A REFRESHINGLY LIGHT LUNCH OR DINNER.

5   medium Moro oranges
4   cups torn lettuce leaves
3   cups rare roast beef strips
1   cup thinly sliced half-rings of red onion
    Citrus Dressing
8   avocado slices

Cut the oranges into halves. Cut the pulp from the white membrane of the orange halves with a small sharp knife. Slice the pulp thinly crosswise. Combine with the lettuce, beef and onion in a large bowl and toss to combine. Pour the dressing over the salad and toss gently to coat. Spoon the salad onto 4 plates. Garnish each with 2 avocado slices. *Makes 4 servings.*

Citrus Dressing

1   Moro orange
$1/3$ cup vegetable oil
1   tablespoon lime or lemon juice
1   tablespoon shredded orange peel
1   tablespoon snipped fresh chives
1   teaspoon sugar
$1/4$ teaspoon pepper

Cut the orange into halves. Squeeze the juice; you should have about $1/3$ cup. Combine the juice with the oil, lime juice, orange peel, chives, sugar and pepper in a jar with a tight-fitting lid. Cover and shake vigorously. *Makes about $2/3$ cup.*

Oroblanco Sorbet

OROBLANCOS ARE ONE OF OUR MOST RECENT DISCOVERIES. THIS SORBET IS INCREDIBLY DELICIOUS DUE TO THE LOW ACIDITY OF THE FRUIT. YOU DON'T NEED AN ICE CREAM MAKER TO PREPARE IT—A METAL PAN WORKS FINE.

$^3/_4$	cup sugar
$^3/_4$	cup water
3	Oroblanco grapefruit, cut into halves
1	tablespoon fresh lemon juice

Combine the sugar and water in a small heavy saucepan. Bring to a boil over medium heat, stirring to dissolve the sugar. Reduce the heat to low and simmer for 5 minutes. Chill in the refrigerator for 15 to 20 minutes, or until mixture is close to room temperature.

Grate 1 teaspoon of grapefruit peel from 1 of the grapefruit. Cut all the grapefruit into halves and squeeze the juice. Pour the juice through a strainer into a large bowl. You should have about $1^3/_4$ cups juice. Stir in the cooled sugar syrup, grapefruit peel and lemon juice.

Freeze the mixture in an ice cream maker according to manufacturer's directions. Serve, or freeze in a tightly sealed freezer container until serving time. *Makes 4 servings.*

TIP: **To make this ice cream without an ice cream maker, freeze the fruit purée in a shallow metal pan until firm. Break up the frozen mixture with a fork. Beat with an electric mixer until fluffy. Cover the mixture and freeze again until firm. You may repeat the freezing and beating steps for a smoother, finer texture. Let stand 15 to 20 minutes to soften before serving.**

Citrus Salad with
Lemon Crème Dressing

2   *Moro oranges, or regular oranges, peeled*
1   *Oroblanco or other grapefruit, peeled*
     Lettuce leaves
     Lemon Crème Dressing

Cut the oranges into halves and cut into thin slices. Cut the grapefruit into quarters and cut into thin slices. Line 4 salad plates with lettuce leaves. Arrange the citrus over the lettuce decoratively. Drizzle the dressing over the salads. *Makes 4 servings.*

Lemon Crème Dressing

$1/4$ *cup light mayonnaise or mayonnaise-style salad dressing*
$1/4$ *cup reduced-fat plain yogurt*
2   *tablespoons minced fresh lemon grass (bulb only)*
1   *tablespoon minced fresh chives*
3   *tablespoons milk*
1   *teaspoon sugar*

Combine the mayonnaise, yogurt, lemon grass, chives, milk and sugar in a blender or food processor container. Process, covered, for 2 or 3 minutes or until well blended. *Makes about $2/3$ cup.*

OROBLANCOS

Oroblancos do everything to the max! They are bigger than most grapefruit, sweeter than most grapefruit, juicier than most grapefruit, and are even more yellow. Developed in 1958 at the University of California at Riverside, the Oroblanco is a hybrid of a pummelo (the original Asian grapefruit) and a regular grapefruit. So grab a spoon and go for the gold!

OROBLANCOS

Passion Fruit and Mango Sorbet

4   ripe, wrinkled passion fruits
3   medium ripe mangos, or large ripe peaches, peeled and chopped
2   tablespoons sugar or to taste

Cut the passion fruits into halves. Spoon the pulp (seeds and all) into a food processor container or blender.

Add the mangos. Process until puréed. Strain out the seeds. Taste the mixture and add sugar if desired.

Freeze the mixture in an ice cream maker according to manufacturer's directions. *Makes 5 or 6 servings.*

TIP: **You can make this sorbet without an ice cream maker. Freeze the fruit purée in a shallow metal pan until firm. Break up the frozen mixture with a fork. Beat with an electric mixer until fluffy. Cover the mixture and freeze again until firm. Let stand 15 to 20 minutes to soften before serving.**

Passion Fruit Daiquiris

$^2/_3$ cup light rum
$^1/_4$ cup lime juice
$^1/_4$ cup sugar
4   ripe, wrinkled passion fruits
2   cups chopped ice
    Lime or pineapple slices for garnish

Combine the rum, lime juice, sugar and passion fruit pulp (seeds and all) in a blender or food processor container. Process until puréed. Strain out the seeds. Return the mixture to the blender. Add the ice and process until smooth. Taste for sweetness and add more sugar if desired. Pour into 6 glasses. Garnish with slices of lime or pineapple. *Makes 6 servings.*

PASSION FRUIT

The biggest berry in the world, the egg-shaped passion fruit has a familiar tropical flavor. Used extensively in "tropical" punches and confections, passion fruit is best experienced fresh. Passion fruit can be purple, yellowish-green, or red on the outside and yellow on the inside. Scoop it right out of the skin and spoon up the jelly-like pulp and the edible seeds. Hint: they are ripe and sweetest when the outside skin is very wrinkled and moldy.

Prosciutto Fruit Salad with Passion Fruit Dressing

THE BLACK PASSION FRUIT SEEDS ADD AN EXOTIC LOOK TO THE DRESSING. THEY RESEMBLE CRACKED PEPPERCORNS.

Bibb lettuce leaves or fresh spinach leaves
2 *ounces prosciutto or ham slices, cut into slivers*
1 *cup fresh pineapple chunks*
1 *cup sliced peeled kiwifruit, melon or peaches*
1/2 *cup cubed Monterey Jack, Muenster or Swiss cheese*
Passion Fruit Dressing

Arrange the lettuce leaves on 4 salad plates. Arrange the prosciutto strips, pineapple, sliced kiwifruit and cheese decoratively over the top. Drizzle the dressing over the salads. *Makes 4 servings.*

Passion Fruit Dressing

2 *ripe, wrinkled passion fruits*
3 *tablespoons olive or vegetable oil*
1 *teaspoon honey*
1/8 *teaspoon pepper*

Scoop out the passion fruit pulp into a blender or food processor container (seeds and all). Add the oil, honey and pepper. Cover and process until seeds are pulverized. *Makes about 1/2 cup.*

Braised Vegetables with Endive

2   or 3 Belgian endives
1   tablespoon butter or margarine
1   tablespoon chopped fresh basil, dill, chervil or chives, or 1 teaspoon dried crushed herbs
$^1/_2$ cup chicken broth or stock
$^3/_4$ cup baby carrots
$^1/_2$ cup pearl onions, peeled, any color
$^1/_3$ cup dry white wine
     Freshly ground pepper to taste
     Fresh herbs

Cut $^1/_4$ inch from the bottom of each Belgian endive. Discard any wilted leaves. Place the Belgian endives in a heavy 2-quart saucepan. Top with pieces of butter and the chopped herbs. Pour the chicken broth into the pan. Bring to a boil, covered. Reduce the heat and simmer, covered, for 10 minutes. Add the carrots, pearl onions and wine and bring to a boil. Reduce the heat and simmer for 15 minutes longer, covered, until all of the vegetables are tender. Remove the vegetables from the pan with a slotted spoon. Sprinkle with pepper and garnish with fresh herbs. *Makes 2 or 3 servings.*

PEARL ONIONS

Two families of Belgian and Italian descent immigrated to California's San Fernando Valley with the secret of pearl onions and shared their first commercial crop with us. Pretty soon, their home garden wasn't large enough to supply all the requests they received, and the pearl onion industry was born. Today, we sell white, red, and gold pearl onions, each with its own distinctive flavor.

Green, White and Orange Veggie Pearls

4   ounces Sugar Snap® peas
1   cup whole peeled baby carrots
12   ounces pearl onions, any color
1   tablespoon butter or margarine
1   tablespoon fresh basil, chopped, or 1 teaspoon crushed dried basil
2   teaspoons chopped fresh thyme or dill, or $^1/_2$ teaspoon crushed dried herb
     Salt and pepper to taste

Cook the Sugar Snap® peas in $^1/_4$ cup boiling water for 10 minutes. Add baby carrots to the peas during the last 8 minutes of cooking. Drain and place in a serving bowl.

Boil the pearl onions in their skins in a saucepan for 3 to 5 minutes or until nearly tender. Drain and rinse well in cold water. Slice off the stem end and slip off skins. Cut any large onions into halves. Add to the serving bowl.

Melt the butter in a small saucepan. Stir in the herbs. Drizzle over the vegetables. Season with salt and pepper and mix well. *Makes 6 servings.*

Shrimp Salad with Dill and Pepino Melon

YOU MAY SUBSTITUTE HONEYDEW OR SHARLYN MELON FOR THE PEPINO.

Lettuce leaves
2 pepino melons, peeled, seeded, sliced thin
3/4 pound large shrimp, cooked, shelled, deveined
1 leek, white part thinly sliced
Dill Cream Dressing

Line a large platter with lettuce leaves. Arrange the melon slices, shrimp and leek on the lettuce. Serve the dressing with the salad. *Makes 3 or 4 servings.*

Dill Cream Dressing

1/2 cup mayonnaise or mayonnaise-style salad dressing
1/2 cup buttermilk
1 tablespoon lemon or lime juice
2 teaspoons chopped fresh dill
2 tablespoons grated Parmesan cheese
1/4 teaspoon dry mustard

Combine the mayonnaise, buttermilk, lemon juice, dill, Parmesan cheese and mustard in a medium bowl and mix well. Use immediately or refrigerate, covered, until ready to use. *Makes about 1 1/4 cups.*

Pepino Melon à la Mode

SERVE THESE SPIRITED PEPINO CHUNKS OVER ICE CREAM, POUND CAKE, OR JUST BY THEMSELVES IN A LONG-STEMMED CHILLED GOBLET.

2 pepino melons
1/3 cup Triple Sec or orange liqueur
1 tablespoon finely chopped crystallized ginger
Toasted slivered almonds

Peel the pepinos and cut into quarters. Carve out the center seed cavity and discard the seeds. Chop the melons into bite-size chunks. Place in a non-metal bowl. Sprinkle the Triple Sec over the melons. Stir in the crystallized ginger. Refrigerate, covered, for 30 minutes to 6 hours to blend flavors. Serve as is, topped with slivered almonds, or over pound cake or ice cream. *Makes 4 to 6 servings.*

PEPINO MELONS

If you were in Chile or Peru, you might ask for a sweet cucumber—that's the pepino. Pepinos, also called melon pears, are football shaped, about the size of an extra-large egg, and are creamy yellow. Some have deep purple stripes. Pepinos are personalized, as one is just the right size for one person. They are very mild, delicate and sweet.

Pasilla-Braised Pork with Plantains

1½ pounds boneless pork, cut into ½-inch cubes
3   cups water
1   cup chopped onion
1   tablespoon chopped fresh oregano
1   tablespoon chopped fresh thyme
2   garlic cloves, minced
¼   teaspoon peppercorns
1   bay leaf
5   to 6 dried Pasilla chiles
2   tablespoons white vinegar
¼   teaspoon cumin seeds
¼   teaspoon ground cloves
2   tablespoons sugar
½   teaspoon salt
2   plantains, peeled and cubed
1   cup water
2   tablespoons chopped fresh cilantro

Combine the pork, 3 cups water, onion, oregano, thyme, garlic, peppercorns and bay leaf in a Dutch oven or large saucepan. Bring to a boil over medium-high heat. Reduce the heat to low. Simmer, covered, for 45 minutes, or until the pork is tender. Drain the pork and discard the bay leaf.

Rehydrate the chiles with boiling water. Drain the chiles, reserving 1 cup of the soaking liquid. Remove the stems and seeds. Chop the chiles finely.

Combine the reserved liquid and chiles, vinegar, cumin seeds, cloves, sugar and salt in a food processor or blender container. Process until puréed.

Add the purée to the pork along with the plantains and 1 cup water. Simmer for 30 minutes or until the plantains are tender, stirring frequently. Sprinkle with the cilantro.
Makes 5 servings.

Spiced Beef with Black Beans and Plantains

THIS STEW HAS CUBAN ROOTS AND IS TYPICALLY FLAVORED WITH CHILES, GARLIC, AND ONIONS.

2   tablespoons vegetable oil
2   pounds boneless chuck steaks, cut into
    $1/2$-inch cubes
2   ($14^{1}/_{2}$-ounce) cans beef broth
1   bay leaf
$3/4$ cup chopped yellow onion
$1/4$ teaspoon pepper
1   tablespoon vegetable oil
1   fresh Anaheim chile, seeded and finely
    chopped
1   to 2 fresh or rehydrated dried Serrano,
    Jalapeño or Pasilla chiles
$3/4$ cup chopped yellow onion
4   garlic cloves, minced, or $1/2$ elephant garlic
    clove, minced
1   tablespoon vegetable oil
2   ripe (yellow to black) plantains, chopped
1   cup diced tomatoes
2   teaspoons capers
11   ounces dried black beans, cooked and drained
1   (2-ounce) jar chopped pimentos, drained
    Hot cooked rice

Heat 2 tablespoons oil in a Dutch oven.
Brown the beef in the hot oil on all sides;
drain. Add the beef broth, bay leaf, $3/4$ cup
onion and pepper. Bring to a boil. Reduce
the heat to low and simmer, covered, for
1 to $1^{1}/_{2}$ hours or until beef is very tender.
Transfer the beef to a plate with a slotted
spoon, reserving juices. Cover to keep warm.

Measure $1^{1}/_{2}$ cups of the pan juices (add
water if necessary) and set aside. Heat
1 tablespoon oil in a large skillet. Add the
chiles, $3/4$ cup onion and garlic. Sauté for
2 minutes. Add 1 tablespoon oil and the
plantains. Sauté for 5 minutes. Stir in the
reserved pan juices, tomatoes and capers.
Bring to a boil. Reduce the heat to low and
simmer, covered, for 15 minutes.

Add the beef and the black beans
and cook until heated through. Taste for
seasoning. Spoon the mixture into a serving
dish. Sprinkle with the pimentos. Serve over
hot cooked rice. *Makes 6 servings.*

Sautéed Plantains

FOR A PRETTY PRESENTATION, SERVE THESE IN A DISH LINED WITH TI LEAVES, WHICH ARE AVAILABLE AT FLORIST SHOPS.

3   tablespoons butter or margarine
2   plantains, peeled and cut into $^1/_2$-inch chunks
    Salt and pepper to taste

Melt the butter in a large skillet. Add the plantain chunks and cook over medium heat for about 20 minutes or until golden, turning frequently. Salt and pepper to taste. *Makes 5 servings.*

PLANTAINS

What can't you do with a plantain? You can slice it and fry or bake it to make sweet or savory chips, boil it and mash it like potatoes, shred it and make plantain hash browns, or bake it with brown sugar and serve as a dessert. Plantains, also called, plátano, can be used at all stages of their ripening. When the outside skins are green, they're starchy and neutral, like a potato. When yellow or black, they are sweet, like a banana.

Aztec Corn Soup with Yuca and Plantains

2   tablespoons butter or margarine
1   cup chopped yellow onion
1   cup sliced celery
1   cup chopped carrot
2   garlic cloves, minced
8   ounces yuca root, peeled, cut into
      1-inch pieces
1   plantain, peeled, chopped
3   cups chicken broth
1   cup water
3   tablespoons lemon juice
1   teaspoon grated orange peel
1   cup corn
$^1/_2$ teaspoon salt
$^1/_4$ teaspoon pepper
$^1/_4$ cup chopped fresh cilantro or parsley

Melt the butter in a large saucepan or Dutch oven. Sauté the onion, celery, carrot and garlic for about 5 minutes or until the vegetables are tender. Stir in yuca, plantain, broth, water, lemon juice and orange peel. Bring to boiling; reduce heat. Simmer, partially covered, for 30 to 40 minutes, or until yuca and plantain are tender.

Remove half of the soup (about 3 cups) to a food processor or blender; cover and process until puréed. Return puréed mixture to saucepan and stir in corn, salt and pepper. Cook until heated through.

Sprinkle each serving with cilantro or parsley. You may substitute $1^1/_2$ cups peeled, sliced sweet potato for the plantain. *Makes 6 or 7 servings.*

Poblano Crab Quesadillas

2   Poblano chiles, rinsed, patted dry
8   burrito-size flour tortillas
8   ounces (1³/₄ cups) fresh or imitation crabmeat
3   cups shredded Monterey Jack cheese
2   green onions, thinly sliced
¹/₄ cup chopped fresh cilantro

Broil the chiles 4 inches from the heat source for 10 minutes or until charred and blistered on all sides, turning frequently with tongs. Place the chiles in a closed plastic bag for 15 minutes to steam. Cut off the stems, remove seeds and veins, then strip off peel. Cut the chiles into ¹/₂-inch-wide strips.

Lay 4 tortillas on large baking sheets. Arrange ¹/₄ of the chile strips across the center of each tortilla. Sprinkle with the crabmeat, cheese, green onions and cilantro, dividing evenly and spreading to within 1 inch of the edge. Top with a second tortilla, gently pressing the tortillas and filling together. Bake at 350 degrees for 10 to 12 minutes or until the tortillas are beginning to brown and the cheese is melted. Cut each quesadilla into wedges. *Makes 4 servings.*

POBLANO CHILES

If you dry a Poblano, you will have an ancho chile. Named for Puebla, Mexico, where it is thought to have originated, the Poblano is dramatic in appearance: long, tapered and dark green. Poblanos have a medium heat, hotter than an Anaheim or a green bell pepper. Poblanos are assertive without being overbearing, and are the traditional chile used for chiles rellenos.

Chile and Corn Rellenos

INSTEAD OF BEING DEEP-FRIED, THESE CHEESE-STUFFED CHILES ARE BAKED IN A HEARTY CORN SAUCE.

6   fresh Poblano chiles
4   ounces Monterey Jack cheese, cut into strips
4   ounces Cheddar cheese, cut into strips
1   tablespoon vegetable oil
1   cup corn kernels, fresh or frozen
¹/₂ cup chopped yellow onion
1   garlic clove, minced
1   cup evaporated milk
2   eggs, lightly beaten
2   tablespoons chopped fresh cilantro
2   teaspoons chopped fresh oregano, or
     ¹/₂ teaspoon crushed dried oregano
¹/₄ teaspoon pepper
2   tablespoons grated Parmesan cheese

Cut the stems off the chiles. Cut a slit down the length of each chile. Scrape out the seeds and veins with the knife. Broil the chiles 4 inches from the heat source, turning frequently, until blistered but not black on all sides. Place the chiles in a paper bag for 15 minutes. Slip the skins off the chiles.

Stuff the chiles with strips of cheese. Arrange the chiles, cheese side up, in a lightly greased 9-inch quiche dish or pie pan.

Heat the oil in a skillet and sauté the corn, onion and garlic for 3 minutes or until the corn is nearly tender. Remove from the heat and stir in the milk, eggs, cilantro, oregano and pepper. Pour the mixture over the chiles. Sprinkle with the Parmesan cheese. Bake at 325 degrees for 30 to 35 minutes or until hot and lightly browned on top. *Makes 6 servings.*

Grilled Purple Asparagus with Camembert Sauce

1   to 1½ pounds purple asparagus,
     stems trimmed ½ to 1 inch
     Olive or vegetable oil
     Salt and pepper to taste
4   ounces Camembert or Brie cheese
1   tablespoon butter
¼   cup dry white wine or chicken broth
1   tablespoon cornstarch
½   cup light cream or half-and-half
1   tablespoon minced fresh chives

Arrange the asparagus on an oiled grill rack or a broiler pan. Brush with olive oil. Season with salt and pepper. Grill or broil for 4 to 6 minutes or until soft and slightly charred, turning once. Transfer to a warm platter.

Remove the rind from the Camembert and cut into chunks. Cook the butter in a medium skillet until it begins to brown. Stir a mixture of the wine and cornstarch into the skillet. Bring to a boil. Reduce the heat to low and stir in the cream and chives. Cook for 2 minutes, stirring frequently. Stir in the cheese and cook until it melts. Serve the sauce over the asparagus. *Makes 4 servings.*

PURPLE ASPARAGUS

How could Frieda's® resist a purple product? Several years ago there was a purple produce craze—we had requests for purple potatoes, peppers and beans. Purple asparagus can be sweeter than white or green asparagus. Peeled and sliced thinly, raw purple asparagus is a good addition to fresh salads and veggie plates. When cooked, purple asparagus maintains its sweetness but changes to a green asparagus color. So show your guests what it looks like before you cook it!

Penne with Purple Asparagus and Sage

HERE'S A COLORFUL, SOPHISTICATED PASTA SIDE DISH. ADD COOKED, SHREDDED CHICKEN OR BAY SHRIMP TO MAKE IT A MAINSTAY.

6   ounces (2 cups) uncooked penne, bowtie or
     rotini pasta
     Salt to taste
1   pound purple asparagus
1½   cups chicken or vegetable broth
½   cup light cream or half-and-half
¼   cup grated Parmesan or Romano cheese
¼   cup shredded Swiss or Jarlsburg cheese
2   teaspoons chopped fresh sage
½   teaspoon salt
¼   teaspoon pepper
1   cup small pear or cherry tomatoes,
     cut into halves

Cook the pasta in boiling salted water according to the package directions until tender; drain well.

Trim the bottom 1 inch of the asparagus spears. Cut the asparagus into 1-inch lengths. Combine the chicken broth and asparagus in a 2-quart saucepan. Bring to a boil. Reduce the heat to low and simmer for about 5 minutes or until tender-crisp.

Drain the asparagus, reserving ½ cup of the broth. Combine the reserved broth and light cream in a saucepan, whisking with a wire whisk. Bring to a boil. Reduce the heat to low and simmer for about 5 minutes until reduced by half, stirring frequently. Stir in the cheeses, sage, ½ teaspoon salt and pepper. Cook until the cheese is melted. Remove from the heat.

Combine the pasta, drained asparagus, tomatoes and cheese sauce in a large pan or serving bowl. Stir gently until vegetables are coated with sauce. Taste for seasoning. *Makes 4 side-dish servings.*

PURPLE ASPARAGUS

Purple Niçoise with Tuna

2   purple potatoes, chopped
     Salt to taste
1   cup cut green beans
1   ripe tomato, seeded, chopped
1/2 cup sliced black olives
1   (6 1/2-ounce) can albacore tuna, drained, flaked
1/2 cup olive oil or vegetable oil
1/3 cup white wine vinegar
1   tablespoon chopped fresh tarragon
1/4 teaspoon salt
1/4 teaspoon pepper
     Lettuce leaves
2   hard-cooked eggs, cut into quarters

Combine the potatoes with salted water to cover in a saucepan. Bring to a boil. Reduce the heat to medium. Cook for 7 minutes or until tender. Drain and let cool slightly. Cook the green beans in a small amount of boiling water in a small saucepan for 5 minutes or until tender-crisp. Drain and immerse in ice water to stop the cooking; drain.

Combine the potatoes, green beans, tomato, olives and tuna in a large bowl and mix gently. Mix the oil, vinegar, tarragon, 1/4 teaspoon salt and pepper in a bowl. Pour over salad and toss. Spoon onto a lettuce-lined platter. Top with the hard-cooked egg quarters. *Makes 4 or 5 servings.*

PURPLE POTATOES

Yes, when you cook purple potatoes they remain purple. So amaze your family and friends with natural purple fries, purple baked potatoes and purple hash browns. Use your purple potatoes wherever you would use a russet potato.

Double Green-Stuffed Purple Potatoes

TINY PURPLE POTATOES, STUFFED WITH A SPINACH FILLING, MAKE A CONVERSATION-PIECE HORS D'OEUVRE.

2   pounds small (egg-sized) purple potatoes
2   cups torn fresh spinach leaves
3   tablespoons sour cream
2   tablespoons grated full-flavored cheese, such as Romano, Gruyère or Cheddar
1   teaspoon lemon juice
1   tablespoon chopped fresh basil, or 1 teaspoon crushed dried basil
1   small garlic clove, minced
     Salt and pepper to taste
     Basil leaves, lemon slices

Cook the potatoes in boiling water to cover in a saucepan for 10 to 15 minutes or just until tender. (Or you may pierce them with a fork and microwave on High for 6 to 8 minutes, turning once halfway through cooking time.) Steam the spinach in a steamer basket over boiling water for 3 to 5 minutes until tender; drain. (Or you may microwave with 1 tablespoon water in covered shallow dish for 1 to 1 1/2 minutes.)

Hollow out a small cavity in the top of each potato with a melon baller or the tip of a potato peeler. Place the potato pulp in a blender or food processor container along with the drained spinach, sour cream, cheese, lemon juice, basil and garlic. Cover and process until blended. Season to taste with salt and pepper.

Spoon the mixture into the potatoes, mounding it on top. Serve as is, cover and chill to serve later the same day or heat in a lightly greased baking dish, covered, in a 375-degree oven for 20 minutes or until hot. Garnish with basil leaves and lemon slices. *Makes 20 to 24 appetizers.*

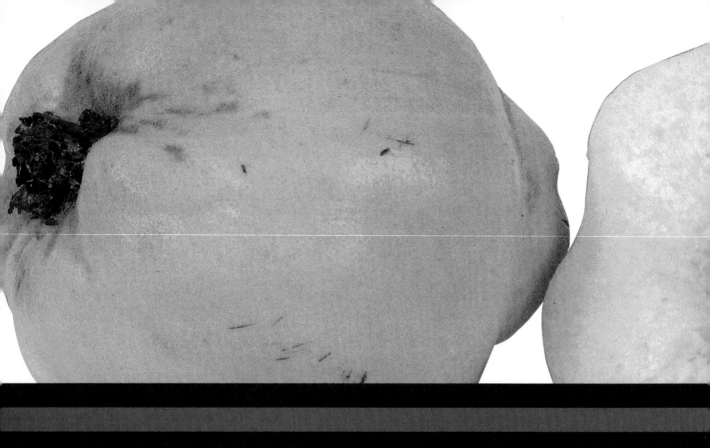

FROM QUINCE

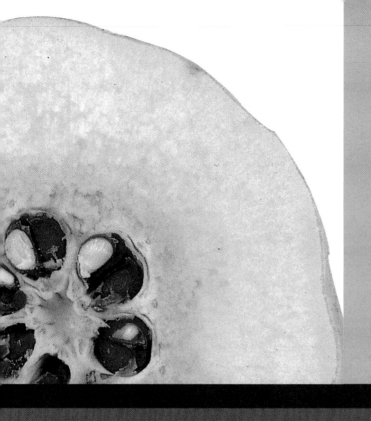

QUINCE
RADICCHIO
RAPINI
SHALLOTS
SHIITAKE MUSHROOMS
SPAGHETTI SQUASH
STAR FRUIT

TO WOOD EAR MUSHROOMS

SUGAR SNAP® PEAS
SUNCHOKES®
SWEET DUMPLING SQUASH
TAMARILLOS
TAMARINDOS
TOMATILLOS
TOMATOES (DRIED)
WOOD EAR MUSHROOMS

Quince Oatmeal Crunch

4   quinces, peeled and thinly sliced
    (about 4$\frac{1}{2}$ cups)
$\frac{1}{4}$ cup apple juice
1   tablespoon lemon juice
$\frac{1}{3}$ cup packed brown sugar
1   tablespoon all-purpose flour
1   teaspoon grated lemon peel
$\frac{1}{2}$ teaspoon pumpkin pie spice
$\frac{1}{2}$ cup dry oatmeal
$\frac{1}{3}$ cup packed brown sugar
$\frac{1}{3}$ cup pine nuts or slivered almonds
$\frac{1}{4}$ cup all-purpose flour
$\frac{1}{4}$ cup cold butter or margarine, cut into pieces

Combine the quince slices with apple and lemon juices in a large bowl and mix well. Stir together brown sugar, 1 tablespoon flour, lemon peel and pumpkin pie spice in a small bowl. Add to the quince mixture and mix well. Spoon the mixture into a 7×11-inch baking dish sprayed with cooking spray.

Combine the oatmeal, brown sugar, pine nuts and $\frac{1}{4}$ cup flour in a large bowl and mix well. Add the butter and cut in with a pastry blender, or two knives used in criss-cross fashion, until the mixture resembles small peas. Sprinkle the oatmeal mixture evenly over the fruit.

Bake at 375 degrees for 40 minutes or until the fruit is very tender and top is golden brown. Serve warm, cool or chilled. *Makes 6 servings.*

Quince Chutney

FOR PARTIES, SPOON THIS CHUTNEY OVER A BRICK OF SOFTENED CREAM CHEESE TO USE AS A CRACKER SPREAD.

$\frac{1}{2}$ cup chopped yellow onion
1   tablespoon vegetable oil
1   garlic clove, minced
1   cup apple juice
$\frac{1}{2}$ cup packed brown sugar
3   tablespoons apple cider vinegar
1   tablespoon lemon juice
1   tablespoon minced fresh ginger
1   quince, peeled, cored and finely chopped
$\frac{1}{2}$ cup chopped dried apricots, apples or
    golden raisins

Sauté the onion in the oil with the garlic in a 3-quart saucepan for 2 minutes. Stir in the apple juice, brown sugar, vinegar, lemon juice, ginger, quince and apricots. Bring to a boil. Reduce the heat to low and simmer, partially covered, for about 40 minutes or until the quince is very tender, stirring occasionally. (Do not allow the liquid to cook away or the mixture will burn.)

Cool to room temperature. Refrigerate, covered, for up to 1 week. *Makes 2 cups.*

QUINCE

Quince, also called membrillo, may look like a golden apple, but you want to avoid taking a great big bite of a raw quince—it can be tart. Quince can be poached, steamed or baked. When cooked long enough with sugar, the quince develops an attractive pink blush. Cooked quince has a mild pineapple-y taste; unsweetened it can be used in Caribbean and African-style stews and in veggie dishes.

QUINCE

Roast Beef Sandwich with Radicchio

RADICCHIO AND GARLIC MAYONNAISE BRING PIZZAZZ BACK TO THE ROAST BEEF SANDWICH.

8   slices sourdough bread, toasted if desired
    Garlic Mayonnaise
1   head radicchio
1   pound sliced roast beef, smoked turkey or
    grilled chicken
6   ounces sliced sharp Cheddar cheese
    Dijon mustard (optional)

Lay the bread on a work surface. Spread each slice with the garlic mayonnaise. Cut the core out of the radicchio. Separate the leaves. Arrange a generous layer of radicchio leaves on half of the bread slices. Top with the roast beef and cheese. Spread with mustard, if desired. Add another layer of radicchio leaves. Top with bread slices, mayonnaise side down. Cut each sandwich into halves diagonally. Serve, or wrap and refrigerate to serve within 24 hours. *Makes 4 sandwiches.*

Garlic Mayonnaise

$2/3$ cup mayonnaise or mayonnaise-style salad
     dressing
5   garlic cloves, minced
1   tablespoon chopped fresh chives

Stir together the mayonnaise, garlic and chives in a small bowl. Chill, covered, until ready to use. *Makes about $2/3$ cup.*

Italian Radicchio Slaw with Bacon Vinaigrette

THE SMOKY FLAVOR OF BACON PERMEATES THE WARM SWEET-AND-SOUR DRESSING IN THIS INTRIGUING SALAD.

1   head radicchio, shredded ($3^1/2$ cups)
3   cups shredded green cabbage
$2/3$ cup pine nuts or slivered almonds, toasted
     Bacon Vinaigrette

Toss the radicchio, green cabbage and pine nuts in a large bowl until combined. Shake the vinaigrette. Pour over the salad and toss to coat. *Makes 4 servings.*

Bacon Vinaigrette

6   slices uncooked bacon, chopped
$1/2$ cup cider vinegar
2   tablespoons sugar
1   teaspoon salt
$1/4$ teaspoon pepper

Cook the bacon until crisp; drain, reserving 3 tablespoons of the hot bacon drippings. Crumble the bacon. Combine the reserved bacon drippings, crumbled bacon, vinegar, sugar, salt and pepper in a jar with a tight-fitting lid. Cover and shake well. *Makes about $3/4$ cup.*

RADICCHIO

There are many different types of radicchio, also called red chicory, which are all the size of a petite head of romaine. All have leaves that are tipped in deep crimson that graduates to seashell pink and ends in brilliant white. Radicchio has a bitter bite, like Belgian endive, and can be braised and served as a cooked vegetable and cut into salads to add a pretty color and flavor.

Millennium Minestrone

1   cup small uncooked macaroni or other small pasta
    Salt to taste
2   tablespoons olive or vegetable oil
1   cup chopped yellow onion
1   cup bias-cut celery
1   cup chopped red bell pepper
1   cup chopped green or yellow bell pepper
5   to 6 cups chicken or vegetable broth
1/2 bunch rapini, cut into 1/2-inch pieces (about 2 cups)
1   (15-ounce) can great Northern or white beans, rinsed and drained
1   medium tomato, chopped
1   tablespoon chopped fresh sage
1   tablespoon chopped fresh basil
1   teaspoon salt
1/4 teaspoon pepper
    Grated Parmesan or Romano cheese as needed

Cook the pasta in boiling salted water according to package directions. Drain and set aside.

Heat the oil in a saucepan. Sauté the onion and celery for 3 minutes. Stir in the bell peppers and cook for 3 minutes longer. Stir in the broth, rapini, beans, tomato, sage, basil, 1 teaspoon salt and pepper. Bring the mixture to a boil. Reduce the heat to low. Simmer, partially covered, for 10 minutes. Stir in the macaroni. Taste for seasoning.

Ladle the soup into bowls. Sprinkle generously with grated cheese.
Makes 5 or 6 servings.

Rapini Stir-Fry with Beef

1/4 cup chicken broth
1   tablespoon oyster sauce
1   teaspoon cornstarch
3   to 4 tablespoons vegetable oil
1/2 bunch rapini, cut into bite-size pieces
1   pound sirloin steak, cut into bite-size pieces
4   green onions, cut into 1-inch lengths
    Hot cooked rice

Stir together the broth, oyster sauce and cornstarch in a small bowl. Heat 2 tablespoons of the oil in a wok or skillet. Stir-fry the rapini for 3 minutes or until crisp-tender. Remove from the wok. Stir-fry the beef and green onions in additional oil until nearly cooked through. Return the rapini to the wok. Stir the broth mixture and pour it into the wok. Cook for 2 minutes longer, stirring, until mixture boils and thickens. Serve over hot cooked rice. *Makes 2 servings.*

RAPINI

Visit any self-respecting Italian or Chinese restaurant and you'll find rapini on the menu. The deep green leaves have tiny flowers that resemble miniature broccoli florets. Rapini, also called broccoli rabe and gai lon, is wonderful sautéed with garlic and olive oil (for the Italian style) or with garlic and peanut oil (for Chinese style).

Fire-and-Ice Fruit and Shallot Stir-Fry

SERVE THIS AS AN EXTRA-SPECIAL SIDE DISH WITH EGGS, CHICKEN OR FISH.

2   tablespoons butter or margarine
1   Asian pear, cored, chopped
1   papaya or mango, peeled, seeded, and cut into 1-inch pieces
6   kumquats, sliced
3   ounces shallots, sliced
2   tablespoons port wine or claret
1   tablespoon honey
    Salt to taste

Melt the butter or margarine in a large skillet or wok. Stir-fry the fruit pieces for 5 minutes or until crisp-tender. Add the shallots, wine, and honey and mix well. Cook over medium heat for about 10 minutes or until shallots are browned, stirring frequently. Season with salt. *Makes 4 servings.*

SHALLOTS

Shallots resemble onions that are masquerading as garlic. The peel is that of an onion and the shape is that of a garlic clove; the flavor is a mild cross between the two. French chefs swear by shallots, claiming they enhance the flavor of every dish in which they appear. An extra-added dividend—shallots are a good source of iron.

Exotic Mushroom Meatloaf with Glazed Shallots

$^1/_2$ ounce dried Shiitake or Porcini mushrooms
$1^1/_2$ pounds ground beef, pork, lamb or turkey or a combination of meats
1   cup (about 2 slices) fresh white or whole wheat bread crumbs
1   egg (or yolk)
1   tablespoon chopped fresh thyme
2   teaspoons chopped fresh sage
$^1/_2$ teaspoon salt
$^1/_4$ teaspoon pepper
4   to 5 shallots, peeled and thinly sliced
$^1/_4$ cup dry red or white wine
    Salt and pepper to taste

Pour hot water to cover over the mushrooms in a bowl. Let stand until softened. Drain and chop the mushrooms.

Combine the mushrooms with the meat, bread crumbs, egg, thyme, sage, $^1/_2$ teaspoon salt and $^1/_4$ teaspoon pepper in a large bowl and mix well. Press the mixture into a lightly oiled loaf pan or a shallow baking dish. Bake, uncovered, at 350 degrees for 45 minutes. Cover and bake for 15 to 30 minutes longer. Remove from the oven and let stand for 5 minutes.

Drain the drippings, reserving 1 tablespoon of the drippings in a small skillet. Heat the skillet. Add the shallots. Sauté for 2 minutes. Add the wine. Bring to a boil. Reduce the heat and simmer for 5 minutes, or until liquid has nearly cooked away. Season with salt and pepper to taste. Spoon the shallots over the meatloaf. Slice and serve. *Makes 4 or 5 servings.*

Mushroom Mignons

2 beef filets mignons
2 ounces fresh Shiitake or Portabello
   mushrooms, stemmed, sliced
2 tablespoons butter or margarine
1/3 cup chopped red onion
1/4 teaspoon Worcestershire sauce
1/4 teaspoon pepper
1/4 teaspoon fines herbes
1/4 cup sour cream

Grill or broil the steaks to desired doneness.
Sauté the mushrooms in the butter with the
onion in a skillet until tender. Stir in the
Worcestershire sauce, pepper, fines herbes
and sour cream. Cook over low heat for
1 minute or until heated through. Serve the
steaks topped with the mushroom mixture.
Garnish the servings with sautéed whole
mushrooms. *Makes 2 servings.*

SHIITAKE MUSHROOMS

**When you reconstitute dried
Shiitake mushrooms, you bring a piece
of the forest back to life: Shiitake
mushrooms are also called "forest
mushrooms." The meaty flavor of
Shiitakes and the broth created by
soaking them fits in well with
vegetarian and meat dishes. We were
lucky to meet Dr. Henry Mee in the
late 1970s when he had perfected a
method for harvesting Shiitakes in six
months, as opposed to the usual two
years. In Asian medicine, Shiitakes are
considered the "elixir of life."**

Fresh Shiitake Mushroom and Onion Tart

MAUI ONIONS ADD A WONDERFULLY RICH, SWEET FLAVOR TO THIS
SAVORY TART. CUT INTO THIN WEDGES FOR AN APPETIZER OR
SERVE AS A SENSATIONAL FIRST COURSE.

   Pastry for a 9-inch one-crust pie
2 cups (2 large) thinly sliced Maui onions or
   yellow onions
3 cups sliced fresh Shiitake mushrooms
3 tablespoons butter, olive oil or vegetable oil
2 tablespoons chopped parsley
1 tablespoon chopped fresh basil, or 1 teaspoon
   crushed dried basil
1/4 teaspoon pepper

Press the pastry into a 9-inch tart pan. Top
with a piece of foil and uncooked rice or dry
beans to weigh down the crust and prevent
bubbles while it bakes. Bake the crust at 450
degrees for 5 minutes. Remove the foil and
rice; discard the rice.

Sauté the onions and mushrooms in
batches in melted butter or oil in a skillet.
Stir in the parsley, basil and pepper. Spoon
the mixture into the crust.

Reduce the oven temperature to 350
degrees. Bake the tart for 25 minutes. Cut
into wedges. You may also use Oyster,
Chanterelle or Morel mushrooms.
Makes 8 servings.

Spaghetti Squash Ring with Green Beans

1   (3- to 4-pound) *Spaghetti squash, cut into halves lengthwise*
1   (7-ounce) can *Mexican-style corn, drained*
$^1/_2$ cup (1 stick) *butter or margarine, melted*
$^1/_2$ cup *fine dry bread crumbs*
4   *eggs, lightly beaten*
1   cup *evaporated milk*
8   ounces *Monterey Jack cheese, shredded*
    Salt and pepper to taste
    French-style green beans, cooked and buttered

Place the squash halves, cut side down, in a large baking dish with about $^1/_4$ inch of water. Bake at 375 degrees for 30 to 40 minutes or until tender. Let the squash cool. Scrape out the seeds. Scrape the interior of the squash and it will separate into spaghetti-like strands. Measure about 4 cups squash.

Combine the squash, corn, butter, bread crumbs, eggs, evaporated milk, cheese, and salt and pepper to taste. Mix lightly but thoroughly. Pour into a well-greased 8-cup ring mold and place in a larger pan. Add about 1 inch of hot water to the larger pan. Bake at 350 degrees for 40 to 45 minutes. Cool slightly before unmolding. Unmold onto a platter and place cooked green beans in center of mold. *Makes 5 to 7 servings.*

NOTE: **You may cook the squash in a microwave oven if you prefer. Pierce the squash in several places with a fork. Place the squash halves, cut side down, in a microwaveable dish with about ¼ inch water. Cover loosely and microwave on High for about 20 minutes or until tender, rotating after 10 minutes.**

Stuffed Spaghetti Squash Italiano

THIS WAS THE FIRST RECIPE WE CREATED TO GO ON OUR LABEL IN THE EARLY 1970S. REMARKABLY EASY TO MAKE, IT IS QUITE FLAVORFUL AND HAS A GREAT TEXTURE.

$^1/_2$ *Spaghetti squash (cut lengthwise), cooked, seeds removed*
1   cup *shredded Cheddar cheese*
1   cup *grated zucchini squash*
1   cup *tomato sauce*
$^1/_4$ teaspoon *salt*
$^1/_4$ teaspoon *pepper*
$^1/_8$ teaspoon *dried basil, crumbled*
    Dash of garlic powder
2   tablespoons *grated Parmesan cheese*

Scrape the interior of the squash with 2 forks to separate the pulp into spaghetti-like strands. Place in a large mixing bowl and reserve the empty shell halves.

Add the Cheddar cheese, zucchini, tomato sauce, salt, pepper, basil and garlic powder and mix well. Spoon the mixture into the empty squash shells. Sprinkle with Parmesan cheese. Place on a baking sheet and bake at 350 degrees for 20 minutes or until bubbly. *Makes 6 to 8 servings.*

SPAGHETTI SQUASH

Spaghetti squash was the first vegetable to make the crossover from the home garden to commercial production. I love to cook up a Spaghetti squash (in a pot of boiling water or in the microwave), split it open, and remove the interior strands that really resemble spaghetti. Imagine a "pasta" with a mild, sweet squash flavor and "al dente" texture.

Grilled Tuna and Star Fruit Salad

1½ pounds fresh tuna, swordfish or salmon fillet,
    1 inch thick, cut into 4 pieces
    Mustard Dressing
2   star fruit, cut crosswise into ¼-inch-thick
    slices
8   cups torn mixed lettuce
1   cucumber, peeled, halved lengthwise and
    thinly sliced
3   green onions, sliced

Arrange the tuna on a lightly oiled grilling tray or broiler pan. Place ¼ cup of the Mustard Dressing in a small bowl. Brush some dressing over the fish. Grill or broil, uncovered, for 5 minutes.

Turn the fish and arrange the star fruit alongside it on the grilling tray. Brush the fish and star fruit lightly with the dressing. Return to the grill. Cook for 3 to 6 minutes longer, or until the fish flakes easily with a fork.

Combine the lettuce and cucumber in a large salad bowl. Add the remaining dressing and toss to coat well. Divide the salad evenly among 4 dinner plates. Place one piece of tuna on the center of each salad. Arrange the star fruit slices around each salad plate. Sprinkle with green onions.
Makes 4 servings.

Mustard Dressing

½   cup mayonnaise or mayonnaise-style salad
    dressing
1   tablespoon lime or lemon juice
1½ teaspoons Dijon mustard
1½ teaspoons chopped fresh dill
¼   teaspoon paprika

Combine the mayonnaise, lime juice, mustard, dill and paprika in a small bowl and mix well. Chill until ready to use.
Makes about ½ cup.

Chocolate-Dipped Star Fruit

3   medium star fruit
1   cup semisweet chocolate pieces
1   tablespoon vegetable shortening (not butter
    or margarine

Wash and dry the fruit. Cut crosswise into ¼-inch-thick slices. Place the slices on paper towels and dry them very well (chocolate will not stick to wet fruit).

Combine the chocolate and shortening in a small saucepan. Heat over medium-low heat until melted, stirring until smooth. Remove from the heat.

Dip half of one star fruit slice into the chocolate until coated, allowing the excess chocolate to drip back into the pan. Place on a waxed-paper-lined baking sheet. Repeat with the remaining star fruit and chocolate.

Chill the fruit in the refrigerator for about 30 minutes, or until the chocolate is set. Serve the day it is made. You may also use white baking chocolate bars for dipping.
Makes 2 to 2½ dozen chocolate-dipped pieces.

STAR FRUIT

Star fruit, also called carambola, really does look like a five-inch-long, five-pointed green or yellow star (depending on ripeness). Star fruit is a native of India and Malaysia and is grown in micro-climates in Florida. Star fruit has an eye-catching glossy skin, similar to the plum in texture, and crisp, sweet interior with a hint of tang. Cut slices of star fruit as garnishes for just about anything, or let the kids use them as edible jewelry!

Curried Chicken with Sugar Snaps

IF YOU LIKE CURRY BUT DON'T WANT TO "FEEL THE BURN," USE THE LESSER AMOUNT.

- $1/2$ cup chicken broth
- $1/2$ cup apple juice or cider
- 2 tablespoons cornstarch
- 2 to 3 teaspoons curry powder
- 1 teaspoon salt
- $1/4$ teaspoon crushed red pepper
- 2 tablespoons peanut or vegetable oil
- 1 pound skinless, boneless chicken thighs or breasts, cut into 1-inch chunks
- 1 tablespoon peanut or vegetable oil
- 1 cup chopped yellow onion
- 1 tablespoon grated fresh ginger
- 1 tablespoon peanut or vegetable oil
- 1 cup julienne-cut red bell pepper
- 1 cup julienne-cut yellow or green bell pepper
- $1/2$ pound Sugar Snap® peas, strings removed
   Hot cooked rice

Stir together the chicken broth, apple juice, cornstarch, curry, salt and red pepper in a medium bowl. Heat 2 tablespoons oil in a wok or large skillet. Stir-fry the chicken over high heat for 3 to 5 minutes, until no longer pink. Remove from the wok.

Add 1 tablespoon oil to the wok. Stir-fry the onion and ginger for 3 minutes. Remove from the wok. Add 1 tablespoon oil and stir-fry the bell peppers for 2 minutes. Add the Sugar Snaps and stir-fry for 1 minute longer. Remove from the wok.

Reduce the heat to medium-low. Stir the sauce; pour into the center of the wok. Cook until the mixture boils and thickens, stirring constantly. Return the chicken and vegetables to the wok. Stir to coat with the sauce. Cover and cook for 2 minutes longer or until heated through. Serve with hot cooked rice. *Makes 4 servings.*

Sugar Snap Chicken Salad in Melon Bowls

- 1 medium melon, such as French Breakfast, Galia, French Afternoon, Casaba, Crenshaw, cantaloupe or honeydew, halved
- 2 chicken breasts, cooked, skinned, julienned
- 1 cup Sugar Snap® peas, halved crosswise
- $1/2$ cup seedless red or green grapes, cut into halves
- $1/4$ cup coarsely chopped walnuts or unsalted sunflower seeds
- $1/4$ cup ranch-style or blue cheese salad dressing
- 1 teaspoon brown sugar
- 1 tablespoon shredded orange peel
   Lettuce leaves such as romaine or salad savoy

Scoop out the melon halves with a grapefruit knife or small paring knife, making $1/4$-inch-thick shells. Cut a thin slice from the bottom of shells if necessary to make them sit securely. Chop the fruit to make 1 cup of $1/2$-inch cubes. Chill the remaining melon for another use. Toss the melon cubes, chicken strips, Sugar Snaps, grapes and walnuts in a large bowl. Stir the salad dressing, brown sugar and orange peel in a small bowl. Spoon the dressing over the salad. Toss until well coated. Line melon shells with lettuce leaves; spoon salad into shells. *Makes 2 servings.*

SUGAR SNAP® PEAS

A cross between English sweet peas and Chinese snow peas, Sugar Snap® peas are crunchy, sweet, refreshing and high in Vitamin C. It was the first veggie to win the All-American seed award. You can eat them fresh or chop them for salads or stir-frys, but I doubt you will have enough left once you've started snacking. Now they're available without strings (stringless).

Sunchokes® Crécy

2   *medium (about 1 pound) Russet or White Rose potatoes, peeled and diced*
3   *large Sunchokes®, peeled and diced (about 1½ cups)*
2   *large carrots, peeled and chopped*
¼   *to ⅓ cup light cream*
2   *tablespoons softened butter or margarine*
2   *teaspoons grated orange peel*
¼   *teaspoon ground nutmeg*
    Salt and pepper to taste

Cook the potatoes, Sunchokes® and carrots in water to cover in separate saucepans until tender; drain. Place all the vegetables in a food processor or blender with cream, butter, orange peel and nutmeg.

Process until smooth and creamy. Season to taste with salt and pepper. Spoon into a baking dish. Bake at 350 degrees for 15 minutes or until heated through.
Makes 6 servings.

SUNCHOKES®

Often called Jerusalem artichokes, these small, knobby veggies were named "Sunchokes®" by my mother, as they are related to sunflowers and have an artichoke-heart flavor. They do not have to be peeled and their nutty artichoke flavor is very nice on veggie platters (dip slices in lemon juice to prevent browning), or use just like potatoes or water chestnuts. Some health authorities have noted that Sunchokes® may be beneficial to diabetics.

Eggplant Stew with Sunchokes®

1   *(14½-ounce) can chicken broth*
1   *small eggplant, peeled and diced*
2   *cups Sunchokes®, julienne-cut*
½   *cup chopped yellow onion*
2   *garlic cloves, minced*
3   *ounces dried tomatoes*
1   *cup chopped fresh tomatoes*
2   *medium green zucchini, sliced*
2   *tablespoons fresh basil, chopped, or 2 teaspoons crushed dried basil*
1   *tablespoon chopped fresh dillweed, or 1 teaspoon dried chopped dill*
    Salt and pepper to taste

Combine the chicken broth, eggplant, Sunchokes®, onion and garlic in a large saucepan. Bring to a boil. Reduce the heat to low and simmer for 15 minutes.

Pour boiling water over the dried tomatoes. Let stand for about 20 minutes or until softened. Drain and cut into slivers. Add the dried tomatoes, fresh tomatoes, zucchini, basil and dillweed to the pan.

Simmer, uncovered, for 5 to 10 minutes more or until vegetables are tender. Season to taste with salt and pepper. Serve with a slotted spoon. Serve hot or chilled.
Makes 8 servings.

Tomato-Scented Sunchokes® with Rosemary and Parmesan

4   tablespoons butter or margarine
1⅓ cups finely chopped yellow onion
1⅓ cups finely chopped celery
12   tomatoes, cut into chunks
¾   cup chopped parsley
1   cup water
2   (6-ounce) cans tomato paste
½   cup fresh chopped oregano, or
     1 teaspoon dried oregano
2   tablespoons fresh chopped rosemary, or
     ½ teaspoon dried rosemary
     Salt and pepper to taste
3   pounds Sunchokes®, peeled if desired and
     thinly sliced
1   cup lemon juice
2   cups grated Parmesan or Romano cheese
18   ounces sliced mozzarella cheese
¼   cup finely chopped parsley

Melt the butter in a medium skillet. Cook the onion and celery until tender. Stir in the tomatoes, ¾ cup parsley, water, tomato paste, oregano, rosemary, salt and pepper. Bring to a boil. Reduce the heat to low and simmer for 10 minutes. Combine the Sunchokes® with water to cover and lemon juice in a saucepan. Bring to a boil, covered. Reduce the heat to low and simmer for 5 minutes; drain.

Spoon 3 cups of the tomato sauce over the bottom of a lightly oiled large rectangular baking pan. Top with an even layer of Sunchokes®. Sprinkle with grated Parmesan or Romano cheese. Top with remaining tomato sauce, spreading to cover Sunchokes®.

Arrange the mozzarella cheese over the sauce. Bake, covered, at 375 degrees for 20 to 25 minutes or until hot and bubbly. Sprinkle with ¼ cup parsley. Cut into squares to serve. *Makes 12 main-dish or 18 side-dish servings.*

Golden Winter Squash Soup

YOU MAY SUBSTITUTE ANY NUMBER OF SQUASH FOR THE SWEET DUMPLING SQUASH. TRY HUBBARD, BANANA, GOLDEN NUGGET, BUTTERNUT, BUTTERCUP, TURBAN, OR KABOCHA. IF YOU LIKE, RESERVE THE SHELLS FOR SERVING DISHES.

1   *cooked Sweet Dumpling squash*
3   *tablespoons butter or margarine*
3   *tablespoons all-purpose flour*
3   *cups milk or light cream*
2   *teaspoons grated orange peel*
1/8 *teaspoon freshly ground black pepper*
1/8 *teaspoon ground mace*
    Orange slices, chopped walnuts or yogurt

Cut the squash into halves. Scoop out the pulp and place in a bowl, reserving the squash shells. Mash the pulp with a potato masher or an electric mixer. Measure 2 cups. Set the mashed squash and squash shells aside.

Melt the butter or margarine in a 3-quart saucepan. Stir in the flour. Add the milk or cream all at once. Cook over medium heat until mixture thickens and bubbles, stirring constantly. Stir in the orange peel, pepper and mace. Place half the squash and half the milk mixture in a blender or food processor. Cover and blend until smooth. Repeat with remaining milk mixture and squash. Return the soup to the saucepan. Cook a few minutes longer or until heated through. If desired, serve soup in squash shells. Garnish each serving with a slice of orange, chopped walnuts or a spoonful of yogurt.
Makes 3 or 4 first-course servings.

Winter Squash with Apples and Wine

2   *Sweet Dumpling or Golden Nugget squash*
2   *tablespoons butter or margarine*
2   *large Jonathan or Golden Delicious apples, cored and chopped*
1   *leek, white part only, sliced*
2   *tablespoons white or rosé wine*
1/4 *teaspoon cinnamon*
1/8 *teaspoon pepper*
1/8 *teaspoon allspice*

Cut the squash into halves. Microwave, cut side up, covered, in a microwaveable dish with 1/4 cup water on High for about 8 minutes, rotating once. Let stand for 5 minutes. (Or, cook the halves, covered, in a small amount of boiling water in a saucepan for 15 minutes.)

Melt the butter or margarine in a skillet. Add the apples and leek. Sauté for 5 minutes. Add the wine, cinnamon, pepper and allspice. Cook for 3 minutes more. Scoop and discard the seeds from the squash. Scoop out the pulp and mash. Add to the skillet and mix well. Spoon the mixture into the squash shells and serve immediately.
Makes 4 servings.

SWEET DUMPLING SQUASH

A Sweet Dumpling squash is also called vegetable gourd, but "Sweet Dumpling" better conveys its very sweet flavor. It is just big enough for one or two people. Bake, roast or microwave a whole squash, scoop out the interior, and use the striped shell as a serving container.

Just-Do-It!
Tamarillo Sauce

THIS SAUCE IS EASY TO MAKE: ALL YOU NEED IS A FOOD PROCESSOR. IT'S GREAT FOR ICE CREAM PARFAITS AND THE COLOR IS VIBRANT!

6   *red or yellow tamarillos*
2   *tablespoons orange juice*
$^{1}/_{2}$ *cup sugar*
1   *teaspoon grated orange peel*

Place the tamarillos in a bowl. Pour boiling water over them. Drain, then slip off the tamarillo skins and remove the stems. Chop the fruit. Combine it in a food processor container or blender with the orange juice, sugar and orange peel. Cover and process until puréed. Refrigerate, covered, for up to one week. *Makes 2$^{1}/_{2}$ cups.*

TAMARILLOS

A native of South America, the tamarillo (say it tam-a-RILL-o) is related to both the potato and the tomato and is considered a fruit. The interior can range from apricot-yellow to deep red. Beware of the deep red variety—the color may wash off hands, but it's almost impossible to get it out of clothing. The tamarillo's tart, almost bitter skin should be removed by poaching or blanching. The aspic-textured interior can be used in sweet-and-sour sauces, chutneys and fruit salads.

Tamarillo Ratatouille

TAMARILLOS TAKE THE PLACE OF TOMATOES, BOTH IN FLAVOR AND TEXTURE, IN THIS EASY VEGETABLE SIDE DISH.

1$^{1}/_{2}$ *cups chicken broth*
1   *small eggplant, peeled and diced (5 to 6 cups)*
4   *tamarillos, any variety, peeled and diced*
1$^{1}/_{2}$ *cups sliced mushrooms*
1   *red, yellow or orange bell pepper, chopped*
1   *clove Elephant garlic, minced, or 3 cloves regular garlic, minced*
2   *tablespoons chopped fresh basil*
1   *tablespoon chopped fresh oregano*
    Salt and pepper to taste
2   *tablespoons grated Parmesan cheese*

Combine the broth, eggplant, tamarillos, mushrooms, bell pepper, garlic, basil and oregano in a large saucepan or Dutch oven. Bring the mixture to a boil.

Reduce the heat and simmer, partially covered, for 30 minutes or until vegetables are tender. Season to taste.

Serve topped with grated Parmesan cheese. *Makes 4 cups, about 6 to 8 servings.*

In-a-Minute Tamarindo-Glazed Chicken

TRY THIS GLAZE ON BARBECUED RIBS OR TURKEY.

2   *tamarindos*
⅓   *cup very hot water*
2   *tablespoons honey*
2   *teaspoons Dijon mustard*
4   *chicken breast halves*

Crush the tamarindo shells with your hands. Discard the shells and threads that run along the pulp. Slit the pulp lengthwise with a sharp knife. Remove the seeds. Place the pulp in the hot water for 15 minutes. Mash the pulp in the liquid with the back of a spoon to release as much pulp as possible. Strain out any remaining seeds.

Stir together the tamarindo liquid, honey and mustard. Bake the chicken breasts in a baking dish at 350 degrees for 30 minutes. Brush the chicken with the tamarindo mixture. Bake for 15 to 20 minutes longer or until cooked through, brushing frequently with the tamarindo mixture. *Makes 4 servings.*

Tamarindo Sauce

1   *tamarindo, shelled*
2   *tablespoons very hot water*
¼   *cup peanut or vegetable oil*
2   *tablespoons soy sauce*
1   *garlic clove, crushed*
2   *teaspoons sesame seeds*

Remove the seeds from tamarindo pulp and place the pulp in the hot water for 15 minutes. Crush the pulp in the liquid with the back of a spoon to release as much pulp as possible. Discard the skin from the pulp. Stir together the tamarindo liquid, oil, soy, garlic and sesame seeds. Try serving sauce over fish, chicken or beef. *Makes about ⅓ cup sauce.*

TAMARINDOS

Resembling a dry, brown-velvet seed pod, tamarindo is popular in Asian, Indian and Latin cuisines. The flavor is sweet, with touches of dates, apricots and citrus. Tamarindo is prized for its pulp, which is used in Latin, Asian and Indian sodas, cold beverages, teas and popsicles. Tamarindo is the secret ingredient in Worcestershire sauce.

Ensalada de Tomatillo

Shredded lettuce
2   cups ½-inch zucchini chunks
2   red tomatoes, cut into wedges
4   tomatillos, peeled, chopped
    Sliced green onion
    Cilantro Chile Vinaigrette

Arrange lettuce on 4 salad plates. Top with zucchini, tomatoes and tomatillos. Sprinkle with the green onion. Shake the dressing. Drizzle over the salads. *Makes 4 servings.*

Cilantro Chile Vinaigrette

½   cup vegetable oil
¼   cup white vinegar
3   cilantro sprigs, chopped
1   Cubanelle or other yellow chile, seeded, chopped
1   garlic clove, minced
1½ teaspoons chopped fresh oregano, or ½ teaspoon crushed dried oregano
1½ teaspoons chopped fresh basil

Combine the ingredients in a jar. Cover and shake vigorously. *Makes about 1 cup.*

TOMATILLOS

The tomatillo resembles a miniature Chinese lantern. Beneath the papery pale-green outer peel lies a perfect, plump green tomato. Acidy and lemony, tomatillos (also called husk tomatoes) can be cut and eaten fresh in salads and gazpacho; boiled until soft; served whole as a vegetable; or chopped and added to sauces, guacamole, green salsas and seafood and poultry dishes.

Corn and Chicken Salad with Tomatillos

THE TOMATILLOS ARE WONDERFULLY FRESH-TASTING IN THIS EASY VERSION OF A MAKE-AHEAD CHICKEN SALAD.

3   cups cooked white or brown rice, cooled
2   cups cooked chicken or turkey, skinned and diced
1   cup niblet corn, no salt added
1½ cups tomatillos, husked and cut into eighths
1   cup diced carrot
    Tomatillo Chile Dressing
    Lettuce leaves

Combine the rice, chicken, corn, tomatillos and carrot in a large bowl and mix well. Pour the dressing mixture over the vegetables. Toss gently to coat. Chill, covered, for 30 minutes or up to 24 hours before serving to allow flavors to blend. Spoon onto lettuce-lined plates to serve. *Makes 6 main-dish servings.*

Tomatillo Chile Dressing

½   cup tomatillos, husked, cut into quarters
½   cup vinegar
2   green onions, sliced
1   Anaheim chile, seeded and minced
1   fresh Serrano or Jalapeño chile, minced
1   teaspoon sugar
¼   teaspoon salt

Combine the tomatillos, vinegar, green onions, chiles, sugar and salt in a blender or food processor. Cover and process until smooth. You may use a dried Chipotle or Ancho chile instead of the Serrano. Soak it in boiling water until softened, then mince it. *Makes ⅔ cup.*

TOMATILLOS

Corn and Chicken Salad with Tomatillos

Dried Tomato Vegetable Risotto

3½ cups low-sodium chicken broth
3 ounces dried yellow or red tomatoes
2 cups diced vegetables, such as zucchini, carrots, red or green bell peppers, asparagus or mushrooms
1 Elephant garlic clove, minced
2 tablespoons margarine
1 cup Italian arborio rice or long-grain rice
1 tablespoon fresh basil, chervil, chives, sage, marjoram or oregano, chopped
⅓ cup grated Parmesan or Romano cheese
   Pepper to taste

Bring the broth to a boil in a medium saucepan. Add the tomatoes. Reduce the heat to low and simmer for 2 minutes. Drain the tomatoes, reserving the liquid in the saucepan. Cut the tomatoes into slivers.

Sauté the diced vegetables and garlic in the margarine in a large saucepan for 3 to 5 minutes or until vegetables are tender. Stir in the rice and tomatoes to coat with margarine. Add 1 cup of the hot broth. Cook over medium heat, stirring constantly, until nearly all the liquid disappears. Then add more broth to barely cover the rice. Cook, stirring constantly, until the broth is nearly absorbed.

Repeat the process, adding broth and cooking the liquid down until the rice is tender and nearly all the liquid has cooked away (about 18 to 25 minutes). Remove the pan from the heat. Stir in the herbs and grated cheese and season to taste with pepper. *Makes 6 servings.*

Dried Tomato and Pine Nut Crostini

THESE DELICIOUS TOASTS SHOW OFF THE RICH, SMOKY FLAVOR OF THE DRIED TOMATOES.

3 ounces dried red or yellow tomatoes
1½ cups diced yellow onions
1 tablespoon olive or vegetable oil
⅓ cup pine nuts
3 tablespoons fresh basil, chopped
1 teaspoon sugar
   Dash pepper
   About 24 thin slices crusty sourdough, French or Italian bread, lightly toasted

Pour boiling water over the tomatoes in a bowl. Let stand until softened. Drain and chop.

Sauté the onions and tomatoes in the oil in a nonstick skillet for about 5 minutes or until tender and lightly browned. Stir in the pine nuts, basil, sugar and pepper. Sauté for 2 to 3 minutes longer. Remove from the heat. Spoon the mixture into a food processor or blender. Cover and process until finely minced. Spread the mixture thickly over the toasted bread. *Makes about 24 pieces.*

DRIED TOMATOES

It takes seventeen pounds of fresh Roma tomatoes to make one pound of our salt-free, preservative-free dried tomatoes. In 1984 I grew tired of using imported, salted, preserved dried tomatoes for recipes and so I went on a search for the perfect dried tomato. We now sell dried Roma tomatoes, dried yellow tomatoes (which look like apricots) and a Tomato Toss™ (sliced dried tomatoes mixed with dried spices and veggies).

Creamy Spinach and
Forest Mushroom Risotto

CHOOSE FROM A WORLD OF MUSHROOMS WHEN MAKING
THIS RECIPE. YOU MAY USE FRESH WOOD EAR, SHIITAKE,
PORTABELLO, OR OYSTER MUSHROOMS. OR USE DRIED
MUSHROOMS, INCLUDING CEPES, CHANTERELLES, MORELS,
PORCINI, SHIITAKE, WOOD EAR, OR OYSTER. LET THEM SOAK IN
HOT WATER FOR ABOUT 30 MINUTES OR UNTIL SOFTENED.

1   (2-ounce) package black wild rice
$^1/_2$ cup long-grain rice
      Chicken broth for cooking rice
       (about $1^1/_2$ cups)
$^1/_2$ (10-ounce) package frozen chopped spinach,
      thawed
2   tablespoons butter or margarine
3   ounces fresh or dried Wood Ear mushrooms,
      cut into bite-size strips
3   shallots, sliced
$^1/_4$ teaspoon nutmeg
$^1/_4$ teaspoon pepper

Cook the rices separately according to
package directions, substituting chicken
broth for water. Squeeze the excess moisture
from the spinach and chop finely. Melt the
butter in a skillet. Sauté the mushrooms and
shallots until tender.

   When the rices are done, stir them
together. Stir in the chopped spinach,
sautéed vegetable mixture, nutmeg and
pepper. Cook for 2 minutes to heat through.
Makes 6 side-dish servings.

Mu Shu Pork with Wood Ear Mushrooms

HERE'S THE TRADITIONAL USE FOR THE INTRIGUING WOOD EAR MUSHROOM. THE TOUGH CENTER PORTION IS THE "STEM." CUT IT OUT AND DISCARD IT.

1   *pound thin-cut boneless pork chops, trimmed of fat*
3   *tablespoons cornstarch*
$^1/_2$ *cup orange juice*
2   *tablespoons soy sauce*
1   *tablespoon hoisin sauce*
3   *tablespoons peanut or vegetable oil*
2   *eggs, slightly beaten*
3   *cups shredded napa cabbage or green cabbage*
4   *green onions, sliced*
1   *cup Wood Ear mushrooms, stems removed, thinly sliced*
4   *to 6 (10-inch) flour tortillas, warmed Bottled plum sauce*

Pound the pork slices between sheets of waxed paper with a meat mallet to a $^1/_4$-inch thickness. Cut the pork into $^1/_4$-inch-wide bite-size strips. Combine the pork and 2 tablespoons cornstarch in a shallow bowl and mix well. Stir together the orange juice, 1 tablespoon cornstarch, soy sauce and hoisin sauce.

Heat a wok or large skillet over high heat. Add 1 tablespoon of the oil. Whisk the eggs into the wok and scramble for 1 to 2 minutes until cooked. Remove to a cutting board and quickly chop finely.

Add 1 more tablespoon of the oil to the wok. Stir-fry the pork for 3 minutes or until no longer pink. Remove from the wok. Add another tablespoon of oil. Stir-fry the cabbage and green onions for 2 to 3 minutes or until cabbage is wilted.

Stir the orange juice mixture. Push the cabbage mixture to one side of the wok. Pour the sauce into the center of the wok and cook until mixture thickens and bubbles, stirring constantly. Add the pork, chopped eggs and wood ear mushrooms and stir to coat with the sauce. Cook, covered, for 2 minutes more or until mixture is heated through.

For each serving, place one flour tortilla on a serving plate. Spoon one-fourth (for 4 servings) or one-sixth (for 6 servings) of the pork mixture into the center of a flour tortilla. Drizzle some plum sauce over the filling. Roll to enclose the filling. Place seam side down on the plates. Spoon more plum sauce on top. Serve immediately.
Makes 4 to 6 servings.

WOOD EAR MUSHROOMS

Wood Ear mushrooms (also called cloud ears) resemble a miniature elephant's ear and are supposed to be dry, brown and rubbery. They have been used for centuries by Asian herbalists. If stored properly, dried Wood Ears will last for up to one year. Reconstitute them to add some "chew" to stir-frys, pilafs, pasta, soups and bean dishes. Wood Ear mushrooms give the classic taste and flavor to Cantonese Mu Shu pork.

ACKNOWLEDGEMENTS

*The following people were
instrumental in the development
of this book:*

Marlene Brown,
who developed the recipes for the book,
is a home economist and cookbook
author who has been creating the
recipes for all of Frieda's products
since 1982. Her latest cookbook is
Great Bread Machine Baking
(Barnes & Noble Books).

Dr. Nancy Berkoff,
who assisted in writing the book, is a
registered dietitian and a certified
chef. She divides her time between
teaching culinary arts and nutrition,
food writing, and consulting nationally
and internationally. Her most
recent book is *Vegan in Volume*,
a vegetarian catering text.

*The work of the following
photographers appears in this book:*

Larry Vogel, Santa Ana, California
Richard Fukuhara, Orange, California
Julie Siegel, Malibu, California

VISUAL GLOSSARY

DESCRIPTION	USAGE	SELECTION/STORAGE

ASIAN PEARS

Apple-shaped with green, yellow, or brown, smooth to bumpy skin; sweet crunchy texture.

Eat out-of-hand, add to salads, bake, poach, or sauté.

Select firm and fragrant fruit; refrigerate up to 3 to 4 weeks.

CACTUS PADS

Green, paddle-shaped cactus leaves with small, prickly thorns.

Remove thorns, chop and add to eggs, omelets, salsas, stir-frys, or casseroles.

Select pads with good color that are crisp and firm; refrigerate up to 2 weeks.

BABY BROCCOLI

Long, slender stems topped with small flowering buds resembling broccoli florets and asparagus.

Use raw in salads, on veggie platters, steam, sauté, or stir-fry; peppery-broccoli flavor.

Select clean, unblemished stalks with full heads; store refrigerated up to 10 days.

CACTUS PEARS

Egg-shaped with prickly skins, light green to magenta; bright-colored flesh with edible seeds.

Peel and enjoy alone, add to fruit salads or blender drinks such as margaritas.

Select firm fruits; ripen at room temperature up to 2 days then refrigerate up to 3 days.

BABY KIWIFRUIT

Fuzzless, brownish-green skin with emerald or yellow flesh.

No need to peel, entire fruit is edible. Add to salads or desserts.

Select firm fruits; refrigerate up to 3 days.

CELERY ROOT

Creviced and knobby with rootlets, can range from apple to melon-sized; white flesh with green stems; celery-walnut flavor.

Peel before using, use raw in salads, add to soups, stews, or boil and mash.

Select unblemished, firm roots that feel heavy for their size; refrigerate up to 2 weeks.

BABY SQUASH

Appearance varies by variety. All are up to 3 inches in length; mild squash flavor.

Steam, sauté, boil, or add to veggie platters for dips, chop into salads, or add to soups.

Select firm, plump, and unblemished squash; store refrigerated up to 1 week.

CHERIMOYA

Somewhat heart-shaped fruit resembling a closed pine cone; white-fleshed, almond-shaped seeds.

Peel and remove seeds; enjoy alone or add to fruit salads. Best served chilled.

Select blemish and bruise-free fruits; ripen at room temperature until soft, chill until ready to serve.

BELGIAN ENDIVE

Closely wrapped, elongated leaves with white ribs and yellow or red tips, 4 to 8 inches long.

Add to salads or use leaves for dips.

Select Belgian endive with smooth, white ribs with no wilted leaves; refrigerate up to 1 week.

CHINESE LONG BEANS

Resembles rough-textured green beans; length can be up to 3 feet long.

Steam, stir-fry, bake, or add to soups or stews.

Choose flexible, unblemished beans; refrigerate in plastic wrap up to 1 week.

VISUAL GLOSSARY

CHIPOTLE CHILES
Brown-colored, smoked Jalapeño chiles, 2 to 4 inches long and 1 inch wide. Heat 5-6 out of 10.

Use in Tex-Mex and Southwestern dishes to add a smoky flavor to sauces and salsas.

Choose clean, even color, and semi-flexible pods; store in a cool, dry place up to 2 months.

ELEPHANT GARLIC
Softball-sized heads or bulbs up to 6 inches across; milder flavor than common garlic.

Roast, bake, or chop to add in soups, stews, pasta sauces, Asian and Latin dishes.

Select plump, firm cloves with unbroken sheaths; store unrefrigerated in a cool, dry place up to 4 weeks.

CILANTRO
Leafy, aromatic herb with slim stems resembling flat leaf parsley.

Season Latin dishes such as salsa and guacamole or Asian stir-frys, soups, and spring rolls.

Select bunches with fresh looking, green leaves. Refrigerate in plastic bag up to 5 days.

FENNEL
Celery-like stems and swollen bulbs with feathery leaves; mild licorice flavor.

Use raw, steam, boil, or sauté, add to soups and stews; use leaves as garnish or flavoring.

Select fairly large, squatty bulbs with pearly sheen; refrigerate up to 4 days.

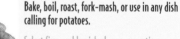

CIPOLLINE ONIONS
Round and flat, 1 1/2 to 2 inches in diameter with a sweet, mild onion flavor.

Roast, broil, or stew, add to casseroles, soups, or barbecue kabob-style.

Select bright clean, firm onions; store unrefrigerated in a cool, dry, well-vented area up to 1 month.

FINGERLING POTATOES
Thin skinned, up to 5 inches in length with fine textured flesh; mild flavored.

Bake, boil, roast, fork-mash, or use in any dish calling for potatoes.

Select firm, unblemished, non-sprouting potatoes; store in a cool, dry, well-vented area up to 1 month.

DAIKON
White, icicle-shaped radish 6 to 10 inches long and about 2 inches wide.

Use fresh in salads or steam for side dish.

Select firm radishes; refrigerate up to 7 days.

FRESH GINGER
Gnarled, knobby root with tan skin and pale yellow to ivory flesh.

Peel and add to stir-frys, soups, and sauces.

Select firm roots; refrigerate up to 3 weeks, store wrapped if cut.

DONUT® PEACHES
White-fleshed Chinese flat peach with a small center stone, 2 1/4 to 3 1/2 inches in diameter.

Enjoy alone or add to fruit salads.

Select firm fruits free from blemishes; ripen at room temperature, then refrigerate up to 3 days.

GOLDEN NUGGET SQUASH
Small, round, hard-shelled, pumpkin-shaped; semisweet squash flavor with a moist texture.

Bake, boil, steam, or microwave, can be puréed or mashed; top with butter, herbs, cinnamon, or brown sugar.

Select unblemished shells; store uncut in a cool, dry area up to 3 months; refrigerate cut squash up to 1 week.

EDAMAME
This soybean is pronounced (eh-dah-MAH-meh) and has a nutty flavor. Pods are tough and hairy.

Remove strings, split pods, and remove beans into a bowl; discard pods. Great as a snack or part of a meal; use in stir-frys, soups, and salads.

Choose unblemished pods and avoid any that are yellow in color. Keep refrigerated in a container for up to 3 weeks.

HABANERO CHILES
Chocolate, orange, red, or yellow; lantern-shaped pods, 2 inches long, 1 1/4 to 1 1/2 inches wide. Heat 10+!

Chop into salsas and sauces.

Choose chiles with smooth, firm, unblemished skin; refrigerate unwrapped up to 2 weeks.

VISUAL GLOSSARY

HORSERADISH

Resembles a tree root 6 to 12 inches long with brown, scruffy, wrinkly skin.

Use raw in meat sauces, salad dressings, or in condiments.

Select firm, unblemished roots; refrigerate in a damp towel up to 3 weeks.

LEEKS

Resembles an overgrown green onion, up to 12 inches long and 1 ½ inches across.

Boil, steam, or chop into soups and stews, may be substituted for onions.

Select leeks with crisp green leaves and firm stems; refrigerate up to 1 to 2 weeks.

JAPANESE EGGPLANT

Narrow, curved shape with dark purple, smooth skin and a soft, white flesh. (At right of photo.)

Can be sautéed, deep-fried, or grilled.

Select firm, glossy-skinned eggplants; refrigerate in plastic wrap up to 3 days.

LEMON GRASS

Fibrous, scallion-like root, gray-green in color with an aromatic lemon flavor.

Use white base portion; slice or grate to flavor soups, sauces, and curries.

Select green stalks with white ended roots; refrigerate in vegetable crisper up to 2 weeks.

JICAMA

Turnip-shaped, light brown covering, 4 to 8 inches across; crisp white to ivory flesh.

Peel and enjoy raw with dips, in salads, or in stir-frys.

Select firm, smooth jicama; store at room temperature until cut, cover with plastic; refrigerate up to 3 days.

LYCHEES

Small, round fruits with tough, bumpy reddish peel with translucent flesh.

Eat out of shell, add flesh to salads, or use in dessert sauces.

Select fruit that has a rosy color; refrigerate up to 2 weeks.

KIWANO®/HORNED MELON

Orange-yellow with spines, 5 inches long and 3 ½ inches in diameter; green, cucumber-like flesh; cucumber-citrus-lime flavored.

Eat directly from shell; top ice cream, desserts, or add to blender drinks.

Select fruits that are free from bruises or splits in outer skin; store at room temperature up to 2 weeks.

MALANGA

Long, curved, or club-shaped with thin, shaggy, brown and patchy skin, light pink interior.

Prepare as you would potatoes; must be cooked prior to eating.

Select firm, unblemished roots; store refrigerated up to 1 week.

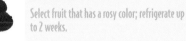

KOHLRABI

Globe-shaped bulbs with stems and collard-like leaves; broccoli-like flavor.

Use leaves and bulbs raw, or cook bulbs like turnips, add leaves to salads.

Select small or medium, unblemished bulbs; refrigerate wrapped up to 1 week.

MANGO

Kidney-shaped green, yellow, or red-blushed skin with a bright yellow, fibrous, juicy flesh.

Peel, remove center seed, enjoy alone or add flesh to salads, salsas, or blender drinks.

Select unblemished fruit; store at room temperature until soft, refrigerate up to 3 days.

KUMQUATS

Kumquats have a tart peel and sweet flesh.

Enjoy kumquats whole or slice into salads or desserts.

Select firm and glossy fruits; store at room temperature up to 2 days then refrigerate up to 2 weeks.

MANZANO BANANAS

Manzanos are short, chubby; skins green to yellow with black spots. (At right of photo)

Enjoy alone, add to fruit salads, or use in recipes calling for bananas.

Select fruits relatively free from blemishes; ripen at room temperature until soft.

MORO ORANGES

Red blushed skin, orange to magenta flesh.

Peel and enjoy alone, add to fruit salads or juice; use as you would common oranges.

Select oranges that feel heavy for their size; refrigerate up to 8 weeks.

POBLANO CHILES

Dark green, wide, tapering pods, 4 to 5 inches long and 2 to 3 inches wide. Heat 3 out of 10.

Thick walls make the Poblano chile great for stuffing, baking, or roasting.

Choose chiles with smooth, firm, unblemished skin; refrigerate unwrapped up to 2 weeks.

OROBLANCOS

Large, grapefruit-sized with a thick, yellow rind; hybrid between a grapefruit and pummelo.

Enjoy as you would grapefruit; low acidity with no bitterness.

Select fruit that feels heavy for its size; refrigerate up to 1 month.

PURPLE ASPARAGUS

Just like common asparagus except for color; purple variety is fruity in flavor and is harvested when only 2 to 3 inches high.

Use whole or sliced fresh, boiled, sautéed, or stir-fried.

Choose fresh, firm spears with closed, compact tips; store refrigerated up to 10 days.

PASSION FRUIT

Round, leathery, purple-brown skin with yellow-ish, jelly-like pulp and edible black seeds.

Use tangy flavored pulp alone, on ice cream, or in blender drinks.

Select fruit that is heavy for its size, pulp is ripe when skin is wrinkled; refrigerate up to 1 week.

PURPLE POTATOES

Small to medium sized with a dark, brownish-violet, thin skin and a bright, purple flesh.

Bake, boil, mash, fry, or use in potato salads; will lose some of the purple color after cooking.

Select firm, unblemished, non-sprouting potatoes; store in a cool, dry, dark, well-vented area up to 1 month.

PEARL ONIONS

Tiny onions typically under 1 inch in diameter, bright colored skins and flesh with a mild onion flavor.

Roast, broil, or stew, add to casseroles, soups, or barbeque kabob-style.

Select bright, clean, firm onions; store unrefrigerated in a cool, dry, well-vented area up to 1 month.

QUINCE

Perfumed variety are football-shaped and tart; Pineapple variety are round/pear-shaped with an acidic pineapple flavor.

Cook before using; use to make jams, marmalades, and syrups.

Select unblemished, smooth-skinned fruit; refrigerate up to 1 month.

PEPINO MELONS

Tear drop shape, green to light yellow and purple striped, smooth skin, 4 to 6 inches in length.

Peel and enjoy or fill halves with shrimp or chicken salads; mild melon flavor.

Select fragrant fruit, free of bruises; ripen at room temperature then refrigerate up to 3 days.

RADICCHIO

Small, tightly packed, thick leaf lettuce with white ribs and red tipped leaves; slightly bitter flavor.

Add to salads, sandwiches, or grill wedges and serve with a vinaigrette.

Select radicchio with smooth white ribs with no wilted leaves; refrigerate up to 1 week.

PLANTAINS

Long, green, thick-skinned with pointed ends; will turn yellow to black while ripening.

Use like a potato-bake, fry, or sauté; must be cooked before eating.

Select plantains that are firm; do not refrigerate until they are at a desirable stage of ripeness.

RAPINI

Dark green, chard-like leaves with tiny buds, slender broccoli-like stalks; bitter flavor.

Steam or boil; add to Italian or Asian dishes.

Select firm stalks with fresh looking leaves; refrigerate in plastic wrap up to 3 to 4 days.

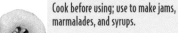
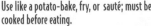

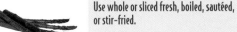

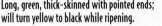

SHALLOTS

Small, oval bulbs in brown or purple sheaths, onion-like cloves with a fragrant, mild, onion-garlic flavor.

Use like onions and garlic in sauces, sautés, or steam with chicken and fish for a side dish.

Select firm bulbs and cloves with papery skins; store unrefrigerated in a cool, dry place up to 1 month.

SHIITAKE MUSHROOMS

Velvety, dark brown or striated caps with light colored stems; meaty texture.

Remove stems; stir-fry, grill, steam, or add to soups.

Select fleshy, firm, dry but unshriveled caps; refrigerate with slightly damp toweling up to 1 week.

SPAGHETTI SQUASH

Football-shaped with a smooth, bright yellow shell; mild flavor with a pale yellow, stringy flesh.

Bake, boil, steam, or microwave; use a fork to separate flesh into pasta strands, top with butter, herbs, or sauces.

Select unblemished shells; store uncut in a cool, dry area up to 3 months; refrigerate cut squash up to 1 week.

STAR FRUIT

Oblong and star-shaped when cut crosswise, 3 to 5 inches long, glossy yellow-color skin and flesh.

Cut crosswise to show star shape; enjoy alone, add to fruit salads, or as a garnish; seeds are edible.

Select firm and unblemished fruit; store at room temperature until semi-soft then refrigerate up to 7 days.

SUGAR SNAP® PEAS

Curved, thick-walled pods approximately 2 ½ to 3 inches long with sweet peas inside.

Use raw, steam, microwave, or add to stir-frys.

Select smooth, bright green pods filled with peas; refrigerate in plastic bag up to 5 days.

SUNCHOKES®

Small, knobby-shaped, thin brown skin with a white, crispy, sweet, artichoke-flavored flesh.

Can be eaten raw, boiled and mashed, roasted, or added to soups, stews, or stir-frys.

Select unblemished roots with smooth skins, no sproutings; refrigerate up to 1 week.

SWEET DUMPLING SQUASH

Scalloped, pumpkin-shaped with creamy white and green striped skin. Sweet squash flavor.

Bake, boil, steam, microwave, purée, mash, or stuff. Top with butter, herbs, cinnamon, or brown sugar.

Select unblemished shells. Store uncut in a cool, dry area up to 3 months. Refrigerate cut squash up to 1 week.

TAMARILLOS

Egg size and shape, glossy smooth scarlet or yellow skin with reddish-orange to yellow flesh.

Peel and cook or use in salads, sauces, or relishes; tomato-tart flavor.

Select firm, heavy fruits; ripen at room temperature until soft then refrigerate up to 4 days.

TAMARINDOS

Brittle brown pods, 5 to 7 inches long that encase large seeds surrounded with a soft, brown pulp.

Pulp can be eaten raw or used to make a syrup for drinks, sauces, chutneys, and marinades.

Select clean, unbroken pods if available; store refrigerated up to 1 month.

TOMATILLOS

Ranges from an inch in diameter to plum-sized, resembles a green cherry tomato but firmer.

Chop for salads or guacamole, slice or dice for cold soups, add to salsas or Mexican stews.

Select tomatillos that are firm, dry, and clean; refrigerate in a paper-lined dish up to 3 weeks.

TOMATOES (DRIED)

Available in yellow or red, chopped or halved. These tomatoes have been seeded and dried.

Add to salads or sauces. To soften, rehydrate in very hot to boiling water for 5 minutes.

Store unopened in a cool, dry place for up to 6 months. Tomatoes will eventually darken but it will not affect flavor. Select tomatoes that look fresh with good color.

WOOD EAR MUSHROOMS

Wood Ears have a very short stalk and light brown flesh that is gelatinous but firm. Dried are more concentrated in flavor than fresh.

Use in soups, sautés, and stir-frys. Add to scrambled eggs or crepe filling.

Store dried in an airtight container for up to 1 year. Refrigerate fresh in a plastic bag and use within 2 days.

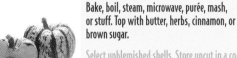

INDEX

INDEX

INDEX

The Specialty Produce People

Try looking for these delicious
specialty produce items at your local
grocery store produce section or visit
Frieda's at www.friedas.com.
Or call us at 800-241-1771.

For additional copies of this book,
please telephone or e-mail us.